T/H/E S/C/O/T/T/I/S/H G/A/S C/O/O/K/B/O/O/K

T/H/E S/C/O/T/T/I/S/H G/A/S C/O/O/K/B/O/O/K

Illustrated by Carola Gordon

RICHARD DREW PUBLISHING

GLASGOW

First Published 1985
RICHARD DREW PUBLISHING LTD
6 Clairmont Gardens
Glasgow G3 7LW
Scotland

British Library Cataloguing in Publication Data

The Scottish Gas Cookbook
1. Cookery
I.   Title
641.5   TX717
ISBN 0-86267-095-0

Printed in Great Britain by
Blantyre Printing & Binding Co. Ltd.

C/O/N/T/E/N/T/S

I / N / T / R / O / D / U / C / T / I / O / N

This cookbook features a selection of recipes recommended by the Home Service Department of Scottish Gas.

Some dishes may already be firm favourites in your household; others, we hope you will find new and exciting. The one thing they all have in common is that they have been tasted and tried by our Home Economists in cookery demonstrations or in their own kitchens.

There are recipes to suit all tastes which range from nourishing economy to sheer extravagance – simple fare for the novice to more elaborate delicacies for the experienced cook. But whoever you are, if you enjoy good food, join us in this GAS-tronomic adventure!

A basic knowledge of cookery is useful because the recipes have been kept as brief as possible, and technical terms have been reduced to a minimum. Who wants to consult a dictionary in the midst of creating a gourmet's delight?

The selection is wide, the ingredients are varied and with the addition of a little imagination, original dishes can easily be created.

The 'proof of the pudding is in the eating' and we hope to encourage readers to try the recipes for themselves. If you have a gas cooker, remember the three zones of heat in the oven. You can cook a variety of dishes at one time by taking advantage of this unique feature. To illustrate this particular point there's a special section at the end of the book entitled 'Dial a Dinner'; here you will find menus and recipes for cooking a complete meal in the oven.

My thanks to all those unsuspecting families, friends and passer's-by, who willingly sampled and commented on, the dishes thrust upon them!

May I wish you 'good cooking' with Wonderfuel Gas.

JOYCE D. FARQUHARSON
Chief Home Service Adviser

He may live without books,
*   What is knowledge but grieving?*
He may live without hope,
*   What is hope but deceiving?*
He may live without love,
*   What is passion but pining?*
But where is the man,
*   Who can live without dining?*

There's nothing more cheering on a cold winter's day than a steaming bowl of home-made soup but a cold soup too can provide a delightful start to a formal meal.

Decorative portions of fish, pâté or mari-nated vegetables are other ways of titillating the palate; the choice is yours from the follow-ing recipes.

Cream of Carrot Soup

2 oz butter	1 pt white stock
2 tablesps grated carrot	1 oz flour
1 chopped onion	½ pt milk
½ teasp. salt	salt and pepper
2 large carrots	parsley
1 bay leaf	

Melt butter in saucepan. Add grated carrot and onion, fry slowly for 5 mins stirring occasionally. Do not allow to brown. Add salt, bay leaf and stock. Cut two large carrots into matchsticks, add to soup, bring to boil, and skim if required. Simmer for 45 mins. Remove bay leaf, blend flour with milk, stir into soup. Boil for 5 mins stirring constantly. Season to taste and serve. Garnish with chopped parsley. **Serves 3**

Gertrude's Lettuce Soup

1 medium sized onion	2½ pts chicken stock
1 lettuce	2-3 sprigs fresh mint
2 oz butter	salt and pepper
2 oz plain flour	sugar – to taste (2 teasps)

Garnish Double cream (whipped), parsley (chopped finely).

Chop onion, fry in butter until soft, but not brown. Add washed lettuce leaves and sprigs of mint, cook quickly until limp, blend in flour then stock. Cook for 10 mins. Allow to cool, put through liquidiser or coarse sieve. Season to taste. Heat before serving. Garnish each serving with a spoonful of whipped cream and sprinkle over finely chopped parsley. **Serves 6**

Cauliflower Soup

1 good-sized cauliflower	1 oz flour
2 pts water	2 egg yolks
1 oz butter	seasonings
2 chicken stock cubes	nutmeg

Break cauliflower into small heads and soak in salt water. Make a roux by mixing the flour and butter in a saucepan, add the stock and stir till it boils. Add the cauliflower and boil for 20 mins. Liquidise or sieve and reheat. Just before serving add egg yolks and seasonings and serve with chopped parsley and fried croûtons. **Serves 4**

French Onion Soup

An authentic tasting short-cut to Soupe à l'Oignon Gratiné. It is always advisable to keep a few canned soups in your cupboard to meet emergencies. And all soups can be perked up by the addition of cream, wine or sherry.

1 medium sized onion, chopped	2 thick slices of French bread
10 fl oz canned condensed onion soup	1½ oz of Emmenthal cheese, grated
5 fl oz dry white wine	½ teasp. grated Parmesan cheese
salt and freshly ground black pepper	

Fry the chopped onion in butter until it is soft. Pour the canned soup and the white wine into a saucepan and heat to simmering point. Add the softened onion and some salt and pepper. Toast the slices of bread on both sides. Pour the soup into two oven proof bowls, add the toasted bread, which should float on top, and sprinkle on the Emmenthal cheese. Place the bowls on a baking sheet in the oven at Mark 8 and bake for about 10 mins, or until the cheese has melted. Sprinkle with grated Parmesan and serve immediately. **Serves 2**

Maincourse Soup

1 oz butter	½ cucumber, diced
1 lb white fish	4 oz canned tomatoes, chopped
1 onion, thinly sliced in rings	½ teasp. salt
1 large carrot, diced	¼ teasp. white pepper
½ teasp. sugar	8 black olives, stoned
1 pt chicken or fish stock	
juice of ½ a lemon	
a sprig of parlsey & bay leaf, tied together	
Garnish Chopped parsley	
grated lemon rind	

Melt butter in pan and fry fish fillets for 2 mins on each side. Lift out and cut into inch-size pieces or flake. Add onions and carrots to the pan and fry for 5 mins, then add cucumber and tomatoes for a further 5 mins. Return the fish and add other ingredients and bring to boil. Simmer for 5 mins then remove bouquet garni. Sprinkle on lemon rind and chopped parsley before serving and serve with hot rolls, or garlic bread. **Serves 4**

Avocado Soup

3 ripe avocado pears	½ pt double cream
1 pt of cold chicken stock	½ teasp. curry powder
1½ pts water	salt and white pepper

De-stone the fruit and scoop out the flesh and liquidise with

the stock. Add the water and cream with seasoning and curry powder to taste. Blend for ½ minute. Serve chilled or heat through slowly, but do not let it boil. **Serves 6–8**

Iced Watercress and Lemon Soup

2 bunches of watercress	1 onion, finely chopped
¾ pt white stock	½ pt skimmed milk
rind of 1 lemon, finely grated	salt & freshly ground black pepper
5 oz carton natural yoghurt	

Wash the watercress and remove excess stalk. Chop the leaves roughly (reserving a few of the best sprigs for garnish) and put into a pan with the onion, stock, milk, grated lemon rind and seasoning to taste. Simmer gently for 30 mins. Purée in a blender or pass through a fine sieve and allow to cool. Stir in the yoghurt, adjust the seasoning and chill. Serve topped with small sprigs of watercress. **Serves 3–4**

Gazpacho Soup

1×15 oz can tomato soup	2 tablesps wine vinegar
2 spring onions	2 tablesps olive oil
1 small green pepper	salt and pepper
2 inch length of cucumber	dash Tabasco sauce

Open can and put the soup into the liquidiser. Chop the onions, pepper and cucumber and add to the soup. Liquidise and then add the other ingredients. Pour into soup bowls. Top with a slice of lemon and chill before serving. **Serves 2**

Consommé Rose

8 small beetroot (raw)	2 onions
2 quarts water	2 cloves garlic
6 carrots	2 egg whites
2 sticks celery	seasoning
3 lbs tomatoes	2 bay leaves

Scrub and peel the beetroot, slice and cook in water until soft. Remove and use in a salad. Allow liquid to cool, then add the sliced vegetables, crushed garlic and bay leaves. Beat the egg whites and add to the beetroot liquid. Bring very slowly to simmering point and simmer gently for about 1 hour. Strain through a linen cloth, season to taste. Cool then chill in the refrigerator. Serve with whipped cream or yoghurt on top. **Serves 6**

Tuna Stuffed Lemons

2 large lemons
7 oz canned tuna fish, drained
2 oz butter
a pinch of dried thyme
1 teasp. Dijon mustard
½ teasp. paprika
salt and freshly ground black pepper
1 egg white
2 bay leaves

First slice the tops off the lemons and set them aside. Slice a little off the other end so the lemon will stand upright. Scoop out all the pulp and place in a sieve resting over a bowl. Press the juice through. In another bowl mash the drained tuna with the butter, then add the mustard and seasonings. Stir in

the lemon juice and finally whip the egg white until stiff and fold it into the mixture. Taste to check the seasoning, fill the lemons with the mixture, replace caps and decorate each with a bay leaf. Chill for 30 mins before serving. **Serves 2**

Shrimps in Sour Cream

8 oz peeled shrimps
5 fl oz soured cream or fresh cream with a squeeze of lemon juice
black pepper
2 oz unsalted butter
2 oz mushrooms
fresh white breadcrumbs

Butter four ramekins and spoon in 2 tablesps shrimps into each. Fry mushrooms gently in butter and put a few into each dish. Season generously with black pepper and cover with sour cream. Sprinkle a thin layer of fine breadcrumbs over the cream and dot with knobs of butter. Bake in the centre of an oven at Mark 5 for 10 mins. Brown under hot grill. Serve with brown bread and butter.

This easily made dish may be served either as a starter or as a fish course. **Serves 4**

Smoked Salmon Mousse

This is a lovely way to make use of those end bits of smoked salmon sold quite cheaply at many delicatessen counters.

4 oz smoked salmon pieces	freshly ground nutmeg
4 tablesps single cream	3 tablesps liquid aspic
1 teasp. lemon juice	1 egg white
salt and freshly ground black pepper	5 fl oz double cream

Chop the smoked salmon coarsely. Put it into a blender or through a food mill, together with the single cream, lemon juice, a little salt, freshly ground black pepper and nutmeg. Blend it into a smooth purée then beat in 3 tablesps of liquid aspic.

Whisk the double cream until it is soft but firm, then fold it into the salmon mixture. Whisk the egg white until stiff but not dry and add it to the mixture. Taste and season again if necessary.

Pour the mousse into a small deep serving dish or individual ramekins and chill until set.

Serve with brown bread and butter or slices of toast. **Serves 2–3**

Scalloped Kippers

1×7 oz can kipper fillets	½ lb cooked, creamed potatoes
½ pt thick white sauce	grated Parmesan cheese
1 teasp. tomato purée	melted butter
1 clove crushed garlic	2 black olives, stoned and halved
pepper	

Mash kipper fillets and combine with white sauce, tomato purée, crushed garlic and pepper to taste. Divide equally between 4 scallop shells. Pipe a border of creamed potatoes round each shell. Sprinkle with grated cheese and melted butter, grill for 5–6 mins. Garnish with black olive. **Serves 4**

Mackerel & Avocado pâté

8 oz smoked mackerel	2 ripe avocado pears
1 tablesp. lemon juice	1 small lemon, finely grated rind
2 cloves garlic (crushed)	1 tablesp. creamed horseradish
2 oz prawns, chopped	black pepper

Remove the skin and any bones from the mackerel, cut into cubes, and place in a blender. Halve the avocados, remove the stones, scoop out flesh and add to blender. Put lemon juice and rind in blender together with crushed garlic and horseradish. Blend all ingredients until smooth. Scoop the blended pâté out into a bowl, fold in the chopped prawns and season to taste.

Place the pâté in a serving dish and chill. Just before serving garnish with unshelled prawns and lemon. **Serves 4**

Covered Pâté

Potato Pastry	
1 medium onion, chopped finely	1 small packet instant potato
6 oz lambs liver, skinned, chopped finely	6 oz plain flour
6 oz sausage meat, chopped finely	pinch salt
1 egg, hard boiled, chopped	4 oz margarine
1 teasp. chopped parsley	
1 teasp. mixed herbs	
1 teasp. lemon juice	
salt and pepper	

Place all ingredients except those for potato pastry into a bowl and mix thoroughly. Make up potato as directed on packet and leave to cool. Sieve flour with salt, rub in margarine until mixture resembles fine breadcrumbs. Add mashed potato and mix well. Divide pastry in two, roll out half on a floured surface and line base of a medium-sized oven proof dish. Alternatively use a 1 lb loaf tin. Add filling. Roll out remaining pastry and cover filling, pressing edges together, decorate as desired. Make a hole in the centre to allow steam to escape. Bake at Mark 6 for approximately one hour until golden brown. Serve hot or cold. **Serves 6–8**

Turkey Pâté

8 oz cooked turkey meat	1 clove of garlic, crushed
4 oz butter	2 tablesps top of the milk
1 onion, chopped finely	1 tablesp. brandy
pinch mixed herbs	salt and pepper

Mince the turkey meat finely. Melt half the butter and sauté the onion and garlic till soft. Stir in the minced turkey, brandy and just enough of the top of the milk to moisten. Season to taste, with salt, pepper and herbs and mix well. Press into 4 ramekin dishes, level the tops and chill. Melt the remaining butter and pour a layer over the pâté and chill till required. Serve with slices of toast or crispbread.
Serves 4 – 6

Chicken Liver Pâté

1 lb chicken livers	2-3 oz butter
4 oz bacon	4 oz mushrooms
2 oz breadcrumbs	seasoning and mixed herbs
2 tablesps brandy	

Sauté livers in half the butter for about 6 mins, mince or chop to a purée. Grill the bacon until crispy then chop finely. Chop mushrooms finely. Return liver purée, bacon and mushrooms to the pan with the remainder of the butter, add the breadcrumbs, herbs and seasoning. Cook 5 mins, stirring occasionally. Add brandy and turn out to cool in a bowl, stirring once or twice as it cools. Place in the refrigerator to chill and set. **Serves 8**

Tomatoes with Sweet and Sour Sauce

4 medium sized tomatoes	1 level teasp. horseradish sauce
4 tablesps oil	pinch each of mustard and sugar
1½ tablesps vinegar	½ oz cucumber
salt and pepper	2 tablesps single cream soured with ½ teasp. vinegar

Remove skin from tomatoes. Make three crossed cuts on the top of each tomato and lift back the flesh like petals. Shake the oil, vinegar, sugar and seasoning together in a screwtop jar. Pour this dressing over the tomatoes, cover and refrigerate for at least one hour. Chop the cucumber very finely, mix with horseradish and soured cream. Serve the tomatoes on a bed of lettuce or watercress and spoon the sauce over. **Serves 4**

Marinated Mushrooms

1 lb button mushrooms	4 tablesps wine vinegar
1 small onion or shallot, (finely chopped)	4 tablesps oil
1 bay leaf	a good pinch of mixed herbs
1 tablesp. tomato ketchup	salt and freshly ground black pepper
1 tablesp. lemon juice	

Wash the mushrooms then put them in a large pan with the lemon juice and cover with water. Bring to the boil; simmer for 2 to 3 mins. Drain them and allow to cool. Put the onion or shallot, vinegar and bay leaf into a small pan. Bring to the boil; simmer gently for 5 mins. Remove from the heat, add the oil, tomato ketchup, herbs and plenty of salt and freshly ground black pepper. Mix well and pour over the mushrooms. Chill for several hours before serving. **Serves 4 – 6**

Minted Grapefruit

2 large grapefruit	2 tablesps finely chopped fresh mint
2 oranges	1 tablesp. lemon juice
8½ fl oz low-calorie lemonade	*To Finish* 4 mint sprigs

Halve the grapefruit, using a zig-zag cut to give a decorative edge. Remove the flesh from the halves. Peel and segment the oranges, remove membranes and cut the segments into pieces. Mix with the grapefruit and return to the grapefruit shells. Mix together the lemon juice, lemonade and chopped mint. Pour into an icetray and freeze to a soft stage. Pile on top of the grapefruit and decorate with a sprig of mint.
Serves 4

Our Main Course selection of recipes range from fish through a variety of meats to poultry and game. Although the number of servings is suggested, a lot depends on the appetite of the diner!

For those who dine alone, many of the dishes are easily adapted to single servings. Alternatively once you have tried a recipe and found it to your liking, why not cook the whole quantity and freeze portions for future use, saving time and money?

F / I / S / H

Salmon Loaf

7 oz tin salmon	1 tablesp. chopped parsley
2 oz soft butter	pinch of salt
1 tablesp. mayonnaise	pinch of cayenne pepper
1 small onion, grated	4 sprigs watercress
1 celery stalk, finely chopped	1 hard-boiled egg

Turn the salmon out into a mixing bowl and mash to a pulp with a fork. Add the butter and mayonnaise and mix thoroughly until it becomes a smooth paste. Add the grated onion, celery, parsley, salt and cayenne pepper and mix together. Press the mixture into a small loaf tin or mould, cover lightly with aluminium foil and chill in the refrigerator for 4 hours. To serve turn the salmon loaf out onto a serving dish and decorate with watercress and the hard-boiled egg cut into slices. **Serves 2**

Fish Cream

6 oz filleted haddock, uncooked	2 eggs
2 oz breadcrumbs	$\frac{1}{2}$ teasp. salt
2 oz butter	pinch pepper
1 teasp. milk	extra breadcrumbs

Cut the fish into strips then chop finely, add to breadcrumbs and season with salt and pepper. Warm the butter and milk together and pour over the fish and crumbs. Mix well and add the yolks of the eggs beaten with one of the whites. Whisk the remaining white till stiff and fold in gently. Pour into greased mould coated with extra breadcrumbs. Cover with greased greaseproof paper and steam for 50 mins. Turn out and serve covered with a parsley sauce. **Serves 2**

Devilled Crab Quiche

8 inch flan case uncooked	
$\frac{1}{2}$ oz lard	
1 small onion $\frac{1}{2}$ small red pepper, de-seeded	finely chopped
2 eggs $\frac{1}{4}$ pt single cream	beaten together
4-6 oz tin crab meat	
2 teasps Worcester sauce	
$\frac{1}{2}$ level teasp. French mustard	
salt, pepper and pinch of cayenne	
few drops of Tabasco sauce, optional	

Melt lard and sauté onion and pepper for 5 mins. Mix remaining filling ingredients and pour into flan case. Bake at Mark 5 for 30–40 mins. Decorate with cucumber slices. Serve hot or cold. **Serves 4**

Grilled Salmon Steaks with Mushrooms

4 salmon steaks	1 crushed clove garlic
1 egg	12 oz quartered mushrooms
3 tablesps olive oil	2 tablesps cream
salt and pepper	juice $\frac{1}{2}$ lemon
fresh breadcrumbs	parsley
3 oz butter	lemon wedges

Rinse salmon in cold water and pat dry. Beat egg with 1 tablesp. of olive oil, salt & pepper. Dip the salmon in egg mixture and then in the breadcrumbs. Heat remaining oil and half the butter. Over fairly high heat brown the steak on both sides 5–8 mins per side. While steaks are cooking, heat remaining butter in another frying pan. Add mushrooms and sauté over moderate heat. Add cream and heat slightly. Arrange the fish on a heated platter and sprinkle with the lemon juice. Surround with the mushrooms and garnish with parsley and lemon wedges. **Serves 4**

Caribbean Haddock

4 oz smoked haddock, cooked and flaked

1 fresh grapefruit

3 tablesps top of the milk

¾ lb mashed potatoes

1 oz cheddar cheese grated

salt and pepper and nutmeg

1 egg yolk

Place segmented grapefruit in base of casserole dish. Mix fish and milk together and place on top of grapefruit. Add egg yolk to mashed potato and season with salt, pepper and nutmeg. Pipe potato round the dish and sprinkle with grated cheese. Bake at Mark 4 for 20 mins and serve with a green salad. **Serves 1–2**

Trout with Apples

4 large rainbow trout, cleaned

freshly ground black pepper

1 tablesp. lemon juice

4 sprigs rosemary

2 oz butter

2 dessert apples cored and thickly sliced

Garnish **1 lemon quartered**

1 teasp. chopped fresh parsley

Sprinkle the inside of the trout with plenty of pepper and the lemon juice and place a sprig of rosemary in the cavity. Use a pinch of dried rosemary if the fresh herb is not available. Fry the trout in the butter over moderate heat for 6 mins. Using wooden spatulas or fish slices, turn the fish over, taking care not to break the skin. Add the apples, cook for a further 6–8 mins, turning the apples once until the fish are just cooked and the apples are deep golden brown. Transfer to a warm serving dish.

Serve the fish surrounded by the apples and garnished with the lemon wedges dipped along the edges in the parsley. **Serves 4**

Crayfish Tails with Tarragon Dressing

12 crayfish tails, fresh or frozen

2 limes or lemons

2 tablesps tarragon vinegar

½ pt vegetable oil

thinly pared rind of 1 lemon

2 eggs, hard-boiled

sprigs of parsley

salt and freshly ground black pepper

sugar to taste

Cook fresh crayfish tails by placing in cold salted water, bringing to the boil and cooking for 10 mins. To cook frozen crayfish, plunge while still frozen into boiling salted water and cook for about 8 mins. Plunge into cold water to cool. Slit the soft undershell of each with scissors and peel away. Ease out the meat in one piece. Slice thickly and return to the shells. Garnish with wedges of lime or lemon.

Put the remaining ingredients into a blender and mix until creamy (or chop the parsley, roughly chop the eggs and whisk with the remaining ingredients in a basin until creamy).

Serve on a platter with salads such as tomatoes and coleslaw, onions and sweet peppers, marinaded mushrooms and cucumber. **Serves 4**

B / E / E / F

Spiced Meat Loaf

½ lb minced beef	1 clove garlic, crushed
4 oz pork sausagemeat	pinch ginger
2 oz farmhouse bran	pinch nutmeg
1 onion, chopped	seasoning
2 oz mushrooms, chopped	2 tablesps stock

Mix together meat and farmhouse bran. Add the onions, mushrooms, garlic and spices. Mix well and season. Moisten with the stock and turn into a 1 lb loaf tin. Bake at Mark 5 for about 1 hour. Leave to cool slightly in tin then turn out. This meat loaf may be eaten hot or cold with salad. **Serves 2 – 3**

Savoury Meatballs

1 onion, chopped
½ lb minced beef
2 oz farmhouse bran
1 clove garlic, crushed
1 tablesp. tomato purée
seasoning
½ level teasp. allspice
¼ pt tomato juice

Mix together meat, farmhouse bran, onion, garlic, tomato purée, allspice and seasoning. Form into meatballs about 1½ inch in diameter and arrange in a shallow ovenproof dish. Pour over tomato juice and bake at Mark 5 for 30 – 40 mins. The mixture may also be shaped into flat burgers for children, possibly omitting the allspice. **Serves 2 – 3**

Country Casserole

1½ lb shoulder steak	6 oz mushrooms
½ lb lambs kidney	½ lb tomatoes
2 oz plain flour	1 large green pepper
seasoning	3-4 sticks celery
dripping	1 tin Royal Game Soup
½ lb onions	1 glass sherry
½ lb carrots	

Prepare kidney and cut into small pieces. Dice steak into 1 inch cubes. Toss meat in seasoned flour and brown in melted dripping. Remove meat from pan. Slice and fry onions until golden brown. Stir in the tin of Royal Game Soup, add washed, whole mushrooms, quartered tomatoes and chopped celery. Bring to boil. Place meat in a casserole and add soup and vegetables. Cover and cook over a low flame for 2 hours, stirring occasionally, or cook in the oven at Mark 1 – 2 for 2 – 2½ hours. Half an hour before serving add blanched matchstick carrots and sliced pepper and a glass of sherry. Serve with rice or noodles. **Serves 6**

Fruit Baked Brisket

3½ lb brisket, boned & rolled	1 beef cube
4 oz dried apricots	dripping
4 oz prunes	2 tablesps vinegar
1 large cooking apple	1 tablesp. brown sugar
2 onions	seasoning

Soak apricots and prunes overnight in ½ pt of water. Remove stones, then mix fruit with peeled, chopped apple and onions. Brown meat in hot dripping, pour off surplus fat. Place meat in casserole and surround with fruit and onion. Combine vinegar, sugar, seasoning and beef cube, pour over meat. Cover and cook in the oven at Mark 2 for 3 hours. Place meat on serving dish. Purée fruit mixture and reheat. Serve sauce separately. **Serves 6 – 8**

Veal Cordon Bleu

4 veal steaks	plain flour
salt and freshly ground pepper	2 eggs, beaten
4 thin slices Emmenthal cheese	2 oz fresh breadcrumbs
4 thin slices cooked ham	6 oz butter
1 large can asparagus tips	

Flatten veal steaks and sprinkle with salt and pepper. Put one slice cheese and 1 slice of ham on one half of each veal steak and fold steak over to encase filling. Pound edges together. Dip into flour, then beaten egg, then crumbs. Press firmly, chill for at least 30 mins. Heat butter in large heavy frying pan and fry steaks for about 8 mins or until golden brown on both sides. Serve with asparagus tips drained and heated in a little butter. **Serves 4**

Escalopes of Veal with Mushroom Sauce

3 oz butter	2 teasps butter
4 thin veal steaks	$\frac{1}{4}$ pt milk
1 small onion, chopped	1-2 tablesps double cream
6 oz button mushrooms	salt and pepper to taste
2 tablesps brandy	2 teasps plain flour

Heat 2 oz of the butter in shallow pan and fry veal on each side until brown, about 4 mins. Remove from pan, add

remaining 1 oz of butter and sauté onion until transparent but not brown. Add sliced mushrooms, cover and simmer for 4 mins. Warm brandy, ignite and pour over. Shake the pan until flames subside. Blend flour with 2 teasps butter, stir into pan. Add milk and stir over gentle heat until the sauce boils and thickens. Stir in cream, season to taste, return veal to pan and simmer, covered, for 5 mins. **Serves 4**

P / O / R / K

Pork and Spiced Plum Casserole

6 pork chops	3 level tablesps demerara sugar
2 tablesps oil	3 tablesps vinegar
12 oz large plums	1 clove garlic, crushed
ground nutmeg	¾ pt stock
6 oz sliced onions	chopped parsley
4 level tablesps flour	

Brown chops on both sides. Stone plums and dust with nutmeg and place round the chops in the casserole. Fry onions till golden, add flour and cook for 1 minute. Remove from heat and add garlic, sugar, vinegar and stock. Return to heat and stir till thick. Pour over chops, cover and cook at Mark 5 for 35 mins. Serve sprinkled with chopped parsley. **Serves 6**

Pork Tandoori

Marinade

10 oz natural yoghurt	4 pork chops
½ teasp. ground ginger	8 oz rice
¾ tablesp. paprika pepper	¼ teasp. powdered saffron or turmeric
1 clove garlic, crushed	
4 bay leaves	
6 peppercorns	
1 tablesp. tomato purée	
grated rind 1 lemon	
1 teasp. salt	

Prick the pork chops well with a fork or a skewer and place in a casserole. Place marinade ingredients in a bowl and mix well. Pour over the chops, making sure they are completely covered. Cover dish and leave for 6–8 hours. At the end of this time baste the chops and remove the bay leaves and peppercorns. Bake at Mark 5 for 1¼ hours basting occasionally. Cook the rice in boiling water with the added saffron or turmeric. To serve, place the rice on warmed serving dish and top with the chops. **Serves 4**

Gammon with Port and Cherries

4 gammon steaks	1 beef cube
2 oz butter	2 glasses port
4 small onions (chopped)	½ pt water
2 teasps tomato purée	cornflour to thicken
2 teasps soft brown sugar	1 × 8½ oz can red cherries

Cook gammon steaks in greased baking dish, covered with foil, at Mark 2 for 30 mins. Melt butter, fry onions until soft, then add tomato purée, brown sugar and crumbled beef cube, and stir well. Slowly add port and juice from cherries, made up to ½ pt with water. Simmer for 5 mins, thicken with cornflour blended with a little water. Gently stir in the cherries, heat thoroughly. Serve the steaks and pour over the sauce. **Serves 4**

Sweet and Sour Spare Ribs

2 lb spare ribs or belly pork	4 tablesps chutney
2 oz butter	4 tablesps thick-cut marmalade

3 finely chopped onions	4 teasps dry mustard
4 tablesps honey or golden syrup	3 teasps paprika
½ pt wine vinegar	salt and pepper
4 tablesps Worcester sauce	

Cut pork into strips (about 12) through crackling and bone. Melt butter in frying pan, fry onion until soft but not brown. Mix all other ingredients, except pork, stir in to onions. Place ribs in shallow roasting tin, pour over sauce. Cover with lid or foil and cook in the oven at Mark 2 for 1½ hours, remove lid for last 20 mins. **Serves 4–6**

Winter Sausage Sizzle

1 small cabbage	1 large onion, cut into rings
½ lb carrots	1 beef cube
1 oz dripping	¾ pt boiling water
1 lb pork or beef sausages	

Wash and shred cabbage. Peel carrots and cut into slices. Put cabbage and carrot in 3 pint casserole. Melt dripping in frying pan, brown sausages and place on top of vegetables, fry onion rings and add to casserole. Finally dissolve beef cube in boiling water and pour over other ingredients. Cover, and cook for 45–50 mins at Mark 5. Serve piping hot with creamed potatoes. **Serves 4**

L / A / M / B

Lamb Kebabs

8 oz lean leg of lamb	1 tablesp. wine vinegar
1 green pepper	salt and pepper to taste
1 small onion, quartered	½ clove garlic, crushed
8 button mushrooms, halved	½ teasp. ground coriander
1 tablesp. olive oil	

Cut the lamb into neat cubes. De-seed the pepper and cut the flesh into squares. Place the meat, pepper squares, onion quarters and mushroom halves in a shallow dish. Mix together the remaining ingredients and pour over. Allow to marinate for at least 2 hours. Thread the ingredients on to a skewer and grill under medium heat for about 20 mins, until cooked, basting with the marinade. **Serves 2**

Rowan and Lamb Chops

1 oz butter
1 onion, finely chopped
2 lamb chump chops
2 tablesps rowan, or redcurrant jelly
pinch of salt and pepper
sprig of fresh rosemary or pinch of dried
¼ pt cider

Melt the butter in a frying pan and fry the onions till soft. Add chops and brown on both sides. Add the jelly, rosemary and cider and season to taste. Cover and cook gently for approx. 20 mins till chops are tender. Turn chops during cooking. **Serves 1 – 2**

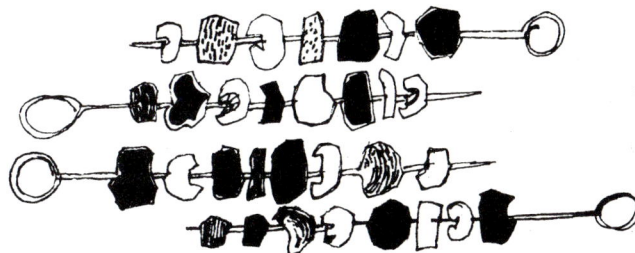

Caledonian Lamb

1½ oz breadcrumbs fresh, white	1 egg yolk
3 oz dried apricots, soaked overnight	2½ lb joint of boned, rolled best end of lamb
4 rashers streaky bacon, de-rinded and chopped	dripping
1 small onion, chopped	*Garnish*
½ level teasp. dried thyme	broccoli, carrots, new potatoes
salt and pepper	

Combine breadcrumbs, chopped apricots, bacon, thyme and seasonings and bind with the egg. Unroll lamb, season well and place stuffing down middle of the lamb. Re-roll, enclosing stuffing and secure with string. Weigh joint and place in a baking tin. Sprinkle with salt and add a little dripping. Cook at Mark 6 allowing 25 mins per pound plus 25 mins over, basting several times. Serve hot with carrots, broccoli and new potatoes tossed in butter and oatmeal. **Serves 6 – 8**

O / F / F / A / L

Crispy-coated liver

3 oz butter	1 egg
1 large onion, peeled and sliced into rings	1 tablesp. milk
1 oz plain flour	1 lb lambs liver, thinly sliced (diagonally)
salt	2 oz rolled porridge oats
freshly ground black pepper	¼ pt chicken stock
1½ teasps mixed dried herbs	*Garnish* sprigs of parsley

Melt one ounce of the butter in a frying pan and stir fry the onion rings over a moderate heat for 5–6 mins. Remove from pan and keep warm.

Mix the flour with salt and pepper and dried herbs. Beat together the egg and milk. Dry the liver slices on kitchen paper. Dip them into the seasoned flour, then into the egg and milk and finally, in the oats. Press firmly. Melt the remaining butter in the pan and when hot fry the liver slices over a moderate heat for about 3 mins on each side, until the coating is crisp and brown.

Remove the liver from the pan and keep it warm. Tip in any remaining seasoned flour and stir well. Add sherry and stock, bring to boil, and season to taste.

Arrange liver on a heated serving dish, scatter the onion rings on top. Serve sauce separately. **Serves 3–4**

Tongue with Almonds

1 ox tongue	*For the sauce:*
1 onion spiked with 4 cloves	1 oz butter
1 sprig of parsley	1 crushed clove garlic
1 tablesp. salt	¾ pt stock, from tongue
1 teasp. oregano	1 tablesp. slivered almonds
6 peppercorns	1 tablesp. chopped parsley
2 bay leaves	

Place tongue in pan and cover with cold water. Bring to the boil and then pour off water. Cover with fresh water and add seasonings, bring back to boil and boil for at least 3 hours, till tender. Allow to cool in liquid then remove skin. Slice tongue and keep warm. Make the sauce by heating the butter and fry garlic for 1 min, add stock and other ingredients and simmer for 5 mins, then boil for 5 mins to reduce the liquid. Pour over the tongue or serve separately. **Serves 6–8**

Kidney Continental

2 lambs kidneys, skinned and cored	½ oz flour
4 Frankfurter sausages	½ oz cooking fat
1 onion, chopped	1 teasp. wine vinegar
¼ lb mushrooms	½ teasp. mustard
⅛ pt stock	1 teasp. sugar
1 dessertsp. tomato purée	

Wash kidneys well. Melt the fat and fry the onions, work in the flour and then the stock. Stir in the purée, vinegar, mustard and sugar and bring to the boil, adding kidneys, sausage and mushrooms. Reduce to simmer and cook for ½ hour. **Serves 2**

P/O/U/L/T/R/Y & G/A/M/E

Pineapple Chicken Salad

1 fresh pineapple	9 tablesps of French dressing
2½ lb cooked chicken	½ level teasp. curry powder
4 oz noodles or rice (cooked)	a little fresh lime juice
8 oz cooked peas	1 lime cut into wedges
4 sticks of celery, sliced	lettuce leaves

Split pineapple in half through the crown to base, cut away flesh, retaining outer shell for serving. Remove core and cut pineapple into 1 inch cubes. Chop the chicken into 1 inch pieces. Blend the dressing with curry powder and lime juice in a bowl, add all ingredients and toss lightly. Chill in refrigerator. To serve, place two pineapple shells on serving dish fill with the pineapple chicken salad. Garnish with lettuce leaves and lime wedges. **Serves 4–6**

Chicken Somerset

a little oil and butter for frying	2 oz sliced mushrooms
4 small chicken pieces	¼ teasp. dried thyme
1 medium-sized onion, chopped	1 bay leaf
1 garlic clove, crushed	salt and freshly ground black pepper
4 slices streaky bacon, chopped	¾ pt dry cider
½ oz butter	
½ oz flour	

Melt some oil and butter in a large frying pan and fry the chicken pieces until golden on all sides. Transfer the chicken pieces to a flame-proof casserole. In the same frying pan (adding a little more oil and butter if necessary) gently fry the onion, garlic and chopped bacon for about 10 mins; place on top of the chicken pieces.

Toss the mushrooms in the frying pan over a low heat for a min. or two then add them to the casserole with the thyme, bay leaf and seasoning. Pour over the cider, bring to simmering point, then cover with a lid and simmer gently for about 45 mins or until the chicken is tender. When the chicken is cooked, transfer it into a warmed serving dish with the bacon and vegetables and keep warm. Work the butter and flour into a smooth paste, then add in small pieces to the cooking liquid and bring it slowly back to simmering point by which time the butter and flour will have melted and thickened the sauce. Taste to check the seasoning, then pour over the chicken. Serve with rice. **Serves 4**

Andalusian Chicken

1 lb cooked chicken, cut into pieces	6 oz brown rice
2 onions, chopped	salt and pepper
1 green pepper, de-seeded and diced	pinch saffron
2 tomatoes, chopped	½ teasp. dried mixed herbs
1 clove garlic, crushed	1 bay leaf
2 tablesps polyunsaturated cooking oil	*Garnish* 1 lemon sliced, parsley.
4 oz packet frozen peas	

Fry the onion, pepper, tomatoes and garlic gently in the oil until soft and golden. Stir in the cooked peas, seasoning and herbs. Cook the rice in ¾ pt chicken stock or water, with the saffron and the bay leaf for about 15 mins or until tender. Drain if necessary (the rice should be quite dry) and remove the bay leaf.

Stir the rice and chicken into the onion mixture and heat thoroughly. Garnish with lemon slices and serve sprinkled with chopped parsley. **Serves 3–4**

Duckling with Honey and Grape Sauce

4 duckling portions	
salt	
Sauce:	
4 tablesps clear honey	**8 oz seedless grapes**
grated rind and juice of ½ orange	**½ oz butter**
Garnish watercress sprigs	

Prick the duckling pieces all over with a sterilised darning needle or fork. Rub salt into the skin so that it crisps well. Place the portions skin side up on a rack over a roasting tin, in the centre of the oven. Cook at Mark 4 for about 1¼ hours or until the meat is tender.

Just before the end of the cooking time, heat the honey, orange rind and juice, grapes and butter and bring the sauce to the boil.

Transfer the duckling to an ovenproof dish, pour over the sauce and return to the oven for 5 mins. Serve hot garnished with the watercress. **Serves 4**

Rum Duck

4 duck portions	3-4 tablesps dark rum
2 tablesps salad oil	**4 tomatoes peeled and chopped**
3 level teasps paprika pepper	**1 green pepper sliced**
1 onion, chopped	**1 teasp. Angostura Bitters**
1 oz plain flour	**salt and pepper**
¾ pt stock	**slices of fried banana to garnish**
boiled rice for serving	**side salad of sliced oranges and onion**

Put oil into a large deep saucepan and blend in paprika. Brown duck portions. Drain and keep on one side. Add onion to the fat and cook till tender. Sprinkle in the flour and stir over a gentle heat for 1 min. Remove from the heat and add the stock gradually, bring to the boil, then simmer for 2 mins, stirring all the time. Stir in the rum, tomato, green pepper and Angostura Bitters. Season well and arrange duck portions on top of the sauce. Cover and simmer gently for 1½–2 hours. Place duck portions on a hot serving dish. Skim the fat from the sauce and pour the sauce round the duck. Garnish with slices of fried banana and serve with boiled rice and a side salad of oranges and onions. **Serves 4**

Roast Duck with Apple and Rice Stuffing

1 duck	¼ pt cider
2 cooking apples	3 onions, minced or finely chopped
4 oz long grain rice, cooked	2 oz breadcrumbs
1 oz butter	1 oz brown sugar
1 oz preserved ginger	pinch ginger
pinch thyme	½ pt stock
1 tablesp. flour	

Peel, core and slice apples and cook in cider for 10 mins until soft, then mix with cooked long grain rice. Cook the onion slowly in butter for 10 mins with the breadcrumbs.

Add spices and season. Stir in the apple and rice mixture and use to stuff duck. Place duck in a little hot fat in a roasting tin. Cook for 10 mins at Mark 7, then reduce the heat to Mark 5. Cook for 15 mins per lb plus 15 mins, basting occasionally. To make gravy, pour off most of the fat from the tin, add the flour and stir till blended over a low heat. Add stock, and a little red wine, if available, bring to the boil and boil for 3 mins stirring continuously. Stuffing may also be cooked separately at Mark 4 until golden and serve topped with bacon rolls. **Serves 4–6**

Turkey in Red Wine Sauce

12 oz cold roast turkey (without bone)	1 tablesp. chopped parsley
1 oz butter	grated rind of ½ orange
½ oz flour	1 bay leaf
1 chicken stock cube	1 sprig of thyme *or*
½ pt hot water	pinch of dried thyme
¼ pt cooking wine	salt and pepper
1 small onion	

Cut the turkey in slices. Peel and chop the onion. Chop the parsley. Grate the orange and wash the fresh herbs. Dissolve the chicken cube in hot water. Melt the butter and add the flour; stir and cook for 1 min. Gradually stir in the stock and wine, stir until it boils. Add the other ingredients. Cover and simmer for ½ hour. Season to taste. Remove bay leaf, add the turkey slices and simmer for a further 15 mins. Any cooked game or poultry can be used instead of turkey. **Serves 2**

Sesame Fried Turkey

2 turkey joints	¼ pt of stock made with 1 chicken cube
seasoned flour	cornflour for thickening
beaten eggs	2 tablesps redcurrant jelly
sesame seeds	2 oz roasted peanuts
oil and butter for frying	

Carefully remove turkey flesh from bones, discarding skin, and cut into thin strips. Dip into seasoned flour and beaten egg and coat in sesame seeds. Chill for ½ hour to set coating. Fry in a mixture of oil and butter until golden. Meanwhile, heat stock (thickened with cornflour) with jelly and peanuts. Pile turkey on to a serving dish and serve with the sauce. **Serves 2**

Venison Casserole

1½ lb stewing venison, cubed	2 carrots, chopped
2 tablesps flour	1 large onion, chopped
1 tablesp. olive oil	1 clove of garlic crushed
1 tablesp. butter	bouquet garni
2 tablesps brandy	½ lb button mushrooms
¼ pt red wine	2 stalks of celery, sliced
salt and black pepper	

Toss venison in seasoned flour. Heat oil and butter in frying pan and brown venison. Place in casserole then add other ingredients to frying pan. Flame off the brandy then add to casserole. Bake at Mark 4 for 2–2½ hours. The length of time depends on the type of meat; farmed venison is more tender than wild deer. **Serves 4**

Game Pie

3 partridges or 2 pheasants jointed and boned	pinch of dried thyme
¾ lb veal, thinly sliced	1 bay leaf
½ lb cooked ham, thinly sliced	1½ oz butter
4 tablesps brandy	3 tablesps olive oil
¼ pt red wine	¼ lb mushrooms, sliced
salt and pepper	½ pt game stock, made from bones
1 tablesp. chopped parsley	12 oz puff pastry
1 small onion, chopped	1 egg, beaten to glaze

Cut the veal and ham into strips. Mix the brandy and wine with the onion, herbs and seasoning and use to marinate the game and meat for 4–5 hours. Sauté the game in the oil and 1 oz butter till lightly browned. Line a deep pie dish with the strips of ham and veal, then add the game and mushrooms, and season with freshly ground salt and pepper. Just cover with marinade and stock and dot with remaining butter. Line the rim of the pie dish with pastry and then cover. Decorate with pastry leaves made from the leftovers and pierce a hole in the centre. Glaze and bake at Mark 7 for ½ hr and reduce to Mark 4 for 2 hrs. **Serves 6–8**

Vegetables add zest and colour to any meal and the vitamins in them do the same for you. Especially when they are freshly picked. Simply cooked and served, nothing could be more delicious.

But when the crop has been excessive and you've frozen all you want to freeze or you are tired of the sameness of peas, beans and mixed vegetables, why not try some mixtures of your own? A few ideas are given in the following section. Some of the recipes are suitable for serving to vegetarian members of the family or friends.

There are also suggestions for salads with a difference – salads for summer parties or winter accompaniments for cold meat and poultry and easy dressings, to suit most tastes.

Brown Rice with Crisp Vegetables

1 medium onion, peeled and sliced	2 leeks, peeled and sliced
1 garlic clove, peeled and crushed	4 oz shelled peas
2 tablesps olive oil	1 oz butter
12 oz brown, long-grained rice	4 oz Cheddar cheese, grated
1½ pts chicken stock, not salted	1 tablesp. chopped mint
freshly ground black pepper	1 tablesp. chopped fresh parsley
1 small cauliflower, cut into small florets	*To serve* grated Parmesan cheese
8 oz carrots, peeled and finely diced	

Fry the onion and garlic in the oil over moderate heat for 2 mins, stirring once or twice. Stir in the rice and cook for 1 min. Pour on the hot stock, add salt and pepper and bring to the boil. Cover the pan, lower the heat and simmer for 40 mins. The rice should be just tender and have absorbed all the stock.

While the rice is cooking, steam the cauliflower, carrots and leeks and peas for about 10–12 mins until they are almost tender. It is very important that they retain their crispness.

Melt the butter in another pan and fry the vegetables, stirring frequently for about 4 mins until they are glazed but not brown. Stir the vegetables, Cheddar cheese and mint into the cooked rice, garnish with the parsley and serve at once. Serve the Parmesan cheese separately. For a perfect accompaniment, serve French bread slit through and spread with garlic butter, then foil wrapped and crisped in a moderate oven for 15 mins. **Serves 6–8**

Spiced Broad Beans with Onions

1 onion	1 clove garlic
salt	1 oz margarine
½ level teasp. ginger	¾ level teasp. cinnamon
½ level teasp. nutmeg	3 lb fresh broad beans

Peel and slice onion. Peel clove of garlic and place on a saucer with a little salt. Using a round-edged knife, rub the salt against the garlic in order to crush the clove. Melt margarine in a medium-sized frying pan, add garlic and onion and fry until onion is golden brown. Stir in ginger, cinnamon and nutmeg, and fry mixture together for about ½ min. Shell beans. Cook in a little boiling salted water until tender, about 5 mins. Drain the beans and stir them carefully into onion and spices to heat through. **Serves 6–8**

Baked Mushrooms with Clotted Cream

1 oz butter	2 bay leaves
1 lb button mushrooms – washed and trimmed	salt and pepper
juice of ½ lemon	¼ pt clotted cream
¼ oz coriander seeds	2 oz Parmesan cheese
fresh chives, chopped	

Melt butter in saucepan, add mushrooms, lemon juice, coriander, bay leaves, seasoning. Cook gently for 2–3 mins. Put mushrooms and juices into an 'oven to table' shallow casserole or individual soufflé dishes. Combine the cream and Parmesan, pour over the mushrooms, cover, cook for 40 mins in oven at Mark 3 uncover for 5–10 mins to brown.

Just before serving, sprinkle with chopped chives. Serve with warm wholemeal or granary rolls for 'dunking' in the gorgeous sauce. Delicious as a savoury served on toast or as a supper dish with jacket potatoes and a crisp salad.

If you are worried about the calories use natural yoghurt to replace the cream. **Serves 3 – 4**

French Beans with Tomatoes

2 oz French beans (topped and tailed)	1 garlic clove
3 large ripe tomatoes (skinned and de-seeded)	salt
1 tablesp. olive oil	freshly ground black pepper

To skin tomatoes, place on fork and hold over gas flame, turning the tomato all the time. The skin will split and is easily removed. Cut the tomatoes in half and scoop out the seeds. Chop the tomato flesh into pieces.

Place the oil in a heavy-based pan over medium heat. When the oil is warm add the beans either whole if small, or cut into 2 inch pieces, and cook for 4 mins, shaking the pan from time to time so that the beans are well coated with oil.

Meanwhile, skin and crush the garlic.

Add the tomatoes. Cook for a further 2 mins, shaking the pan from time to time.

When the beans and tomatoes are bubbling gently, add the garlic and salt. Reduce the heat, cover the pan and simmer gently for a further 6 mins.

Season with freshly ground black pepper just before serving, can be eaten hot or cold. **Serves 1 – 2**

Soufflé Jacket Potatoes

2 medium potatoes	2 egg yolks
1 oz margarine or butter	1 tablesp. of milk
seasoning	2 oz grated Cheddar or Gruyère cheese

Bake the potatoes in their jackets for about 1 hour in a moderately hot oven Mark 5. Split through the centre, scoop the pulp into a basin and mash with the margarine or butter and seasoning. Separate eggs and beat the yolks, milk and cheese into the potato mixture. Serve immediately. **Serves 2**

Potato Mushroom Bake

4 oz vegetable margarine	1 teasp. mixed herbs
3 large onions	1 teasp. paprika
1 lb small mushrooms	1 teasp. sugar
1 red pepper	1 tablesp. soy sauce
4 tablesps wholemeal plain flour	vegetable salt
2 cups stock or water	1 oz Cheddar cheese

Potato Topping

1 lb old potatoes	3 tablesps milk
1 oz vegetable margarine	

Heat 2 oz margarine in large pan, add peeled and roughly chopped onions; sauté gently until onions are light golden brown. Add halved mushrooms and seeded and cubed red pepper, sauté for 5 mins, stirring occasionally. Remove vegetables from pan. Melt remaining margarine in pan; add flour, gradually stir in stock or water. Bring to boil stirring until sauce thickens. Add herbs, paprika, raw sugar, soy sauce and salt; stir until combined. Return vegetables to pan; reduce heat; simmer covered 10 mins. Put mixture into an ovenproof dish.

Potato topping: Peel potatoes, cook until tender, drain and dry. Sieve into bowl and beat in margarine and milk. Cover cooked vegetables with potato, sprinkle over grated cheese and bake at Mark 6 for 20 – 25 mins, until heated through and topping is golden brown. **Serves 4 – 6**

Sprouts with Chestnuts

For every 1 lb of cooked sprouts allow ½ lb of cooked peeled chestnuts, coarsely chopped. Melt butter in a frying pan, toss in the sprouts and chestnut and stir fry until nicely brown. **Serves 4**

Fluellen's pie

9 inch pastry case (cooked)	2 oz grated cheese
1 oz cornflour	8 small leeks
1 oz butter	*Garnish* bacon rolls
½ pt milk	tomatoes
seasonings	parsley

Make white sauce. Add half of the grated cheese. Sauté leeks. Chop two and add to sauce. Turn into pastry case. Use other leeks to section pie. Sprinkle with remainder of grated cheese and grill lightly. **Serves 4**

Casablanca Casserole

1 onion, chopped	1 teasp. ground ginger
2 garlic cloves, crushed	4 whole cloves
1 green pepper, chopped	2 teasps sea salt
½ lb shredded cabbage	1 tablesp. pepper
4 tablesps soya sauce	4 oz raisins
¼ cup water	1 lb sliced tomatoes
3 tablesps oil	½ lb chick peas, cooked

Sauté the onion, garlic and green pepper in the oil until tender, then add the cabbage and cook for a further 10 mins. Dilute the soya sauce in the water. Add the ginger, cloves, sea salt, pepper and raisins to the vegetable mixture and mix well. Then stir in the tomatoes and the chick peas. Transfer this to a greased casserole and pour on the soya sauce. Bake for 25–30 mins at Mark 4 and serve with a sprinkling of parsley. **Serves 4**

Quick Pepper Savoury

2 large onions, peeled	2 tablesps sunflower seeds
4 large green peppers	1 teasp. cinnamon
1 clove garlic, crushed	sea salt
2 oz butter or 3 tablesps oil	1 × 5 oz carton soured cream
1 × 14 oz can tomatoes	2 tablesps skimmed milk powder
soft wholewheat breadcrumbs	

Slice onion and peppers discarding pepper seeds. Using a pan or flameproof casserole, fry onions, peppers and garlic in the fat until tender, then add the tomatoes and sunflower seeds. Season with cinnamon and salt. Mix together soured cream and milk powder, then pour over the pepper mixture, top with breadcrumbs and dots of butter and put under grill until golden and crispy. **Serves 4**

S/A/L/A/D/S A/N/D D/R/E/S/S/I/N/G/S

Easy Dressings:

Quick Mayonnaise

1 whole egg	½ pt oil – olive oil or half olive oil, half vegetable oil
1 teasp. sea salt	2 tablesps wine vinegar or lemon juice
½ teasp. sugar	1 teasp. mustard

Break egg (which should be at room temperature) into liquidiser, beat thoroughly with the sea salt, sugar and mustard. Add oil, a little at a time until mixture begins to thicken, then add more quickly to make a smooth, thick mayonnaise. Finally mix in vinegar or lemon juice. In a cool place this will keep for a week, at least.

Vinaigrette

| 2 tablesps wine vinegar or lemon juice | 6 tablesps olive oil or vegetable oil |
| sea salt, pepper | |

Whisk, shake or liquidise all together. This dressing may be made up in quantity and stored in a screw-top jar in the fridge where it will keep indefinitely.

Alfalfa Slaw

| 1 lb grated cabbage | 1 cup alfalfa sprouts (bean sprouts) |
| 2 carrots, grated | vinaigrette |

Mix together all the vegetables; add enough vinaigrette to moisten. **Serves 6 – 8**

Orange, Cucumber and Mint Salad

| 2 large oranges | chopped fresh mint |
| ½ cucumber | |

Remove peel and pith from the oranges; slice flesh into rings. Slice cucumber. Arrange on dishes and sprinkle with chopped mint. Very refreshing. **Serves 2 – 3**

Pineapple and Cream Cheese Salad

4 slices fresh pineapple	toasted flaked almonds
lettuce leaves	black grapes to decorate
12 oz cream cheese	

Skin and core pineapple slices and arrange on lettuce; pile up with cream cheese, sprinkle with nuts and decorate with halved black grapes. **Serves 4**

Cucumber and Grape Salad

Marinade

1 large cucumber, peeled and thinly sliced	3 tablesps olive oil
1 lb green grapes, washed, halved and seeded	1 tablesp. wine vinegar
$\frac{1}{2}$ pt water	$\frac{1}{4}$ teasp. salt
5 oz packet lemon jelly	$\frac{1}{4}$ teasp. black pepper
3 tablesps orange juice	$\frac{1}{4}$ teasp. dry mustard
5 tablesps lemon juice	
1 tablesp. very finely chopped onion	
$\frac{1}{8}$ teasp. cayenne pepper	
$\frac{1}{2}$ teasp. salt	
$\frac{1}{4}$ teasp. white pepper	
1 lettuce, washed and shredded	

Combine all ingredients for marinade in a medium sized bowl. Place the cucumber slices and grapes in the marinade for at least 30 mins.

Boil $\frac{1}{4}$ pt water, remove from heat and add jelly. Dissolve and add remaining water. Stir in the orange and lemon juice, onion, pepper and salt. Cool the jelly until it is almost set. Remove cucumber and grapes from marinade, drain thoroughly and add most of them to jelly. Reserve the marinade and remaining grapes and cucumber for garnish. Spoon the jelly into a $2\frac{1}{2}$ pt mould. Cover with foil and put in the refrigerator until set. (3–4 hours)

Arrange the lettuce on a serving dish. Turn out the jelly on to the lettuce. Arrange the reserved grapes and cucumber slices around the salad and pour a little of the reserved marinade over them.

Serve at once. **Serves 6–8**

Fennel and Apple Salad

2 medium-sized roots of fennel, trimmed and thinly-sliced
2 red-skinned dessert apples, cored and thinly sliced
2 tablesps seedless raisins, to garnish

Dressing

$\frac{1}{4}$ pt soured cream	1 tablesp. orange juice
1 teasp. cider vinegar	pinch of sugar
grated rind of $\frac{1}{2}$ orange	salt and ground black pepper

Dressing: Mix together all ingredients, taste and season. Toss fennel and apples in the dressing. Garnish with raisins. **Serves 4–6**

Avocado Dip

1 large ripe avocado	2 teasps lemon juice
$\frac{1}{4}$ pt mayonnaise	1 tablesp. brandy
$\frac{1}{4}$ pt sour cream	1 teasp. sugar
1 teasp. French mustard	salt and pepper

Remove seed and skin from avocado; put all flesh into electric blender. Add mayonnaise, mustard, lemon juice, sour cream, salt, pepper, brandy and sugar; blend on medium speed 1 min or until very smooth. Cover; refrigerate. (Make only 30 mins before using or avocado may turn brown).

Prepare raw vegetables to dip. For example; florets of cauliflower, carrot and celery sticks, chicory leaves, potato crisps or small crackers. **Serves 4–6**

Grannies Texas Coleslaw

1 small head cabbage, finely shredded

Dressing

¼ pt sour cream	**¼ teasp. salt**
¼ pt vinegar	**1 teasp. mustard**
1 egg, well beaten	**2 tablesps flour mixed with a little milk**
½ teasp. butter	

Mix all dressing ingredients together and boil, stirring constantly. Pour over finely shredded cabbage, while very hot, stir well then set aside to cool. **Serves 6–8**

Summer Salad

1 small cucumber	**salt and black pepper**
12 large strawberries	**1-2 tablesps Cinzano Extra Dry**

Peel the cucumber and slice it thinly. Wash, hull and drain strawberries. Cut them into thin, even slices. Arrange the slices in a decorative pattern in a shallow serving dish – an outer circle of cucumber, slightly overlapped by a circle of strawberries, then a circle of cucumber, finishing with a centre of strawberry slices. Season lightly with salt and pepper, sprinkle with Cinzano and chill in the refrigerator before serving. **Serves 4**

Greek Island Salad

3 oz fetta cheese	**3 large tomatoes, thinly sliced**
1 onion, thinly sliced	**6-8 black olives**
1 medium sliced gherkin	**½ teasp. coriander seeds finely crushed**
1 clove garlic, crushed	**2 tablesps olive oil**
½ teasp. oregano	**salt and freshly ground black pepper**

Cut the cheese into fairly thin strips, 1½ inches long. Place cheese in salad bowl, add tomatoes, onion rings, olives and gherkin, mix together. In a small bowl combine the garlic, herbs and olive oil, pour over salad. Season and serve.
Serves 3

Canton Caprice

6-8 Chinese leaves	**6 slices cucumber**
1 dessert apple	**4 tablesps mayonnaise**
3 spring onions	**2 tablesps vinaigrette dressing**
2 sticks celery	**salt and pepper**

Wash and dry Chinese leaves, remove part of centre stem from each leaf, a triangle approx. 3 inches from apex to base, should be removed; this could be cut into sticks for avocado dip. Slice the leaves finely by stacking them on top of each other and cutting across the leaves in very fine strips. Place in a bowl, peel and grate the apple into the same bowl, chop spring onions and celery and add with cucumber slices cut into strips. Mix all together. Combine mayonnaise and vinaigrette dressing, season and stir into salad ingredients. Chill and serve. **Serves 4–6**

N.B. Salad cream mixed with 2 tablesps milk can be used if time is short.

For those with a 'sweet tooth' this is the most important part of a cookery book. However, slimmers beware, these recipes are not for you – unless, a tiny portion of Iced Pineapple Liqueur or a spoonful of Prune and Apricot Ginger Compote?

Hot and cold puddings and desserts for all the family, some quick to prepare, others take a little more time but all so tempting. The decision is – which one to try first?

Embassy Pudding

Pastry	Filling
1 oz ground almonds	2 tablesps raisins
5 oz plain flour	little hot water
3 oz butter	3 oz mixed glacé fruits
1 egg	2 tablesps kirsch or rum
little cold water to mix	1 pt milk
	1 teasp. vanilla essence
	2 eggs plus 1 egg yolk
	2 oz sugar
Decoration	grated nutmeg
12 glacé cherries	

Make pastry in usual way, line an 8 inch flan ring and bake 'blind'. Soak the raisins in hot water for 5 mins, drain well. Chop glacé fruits and mix with raisins and kirsch or rum. Let mixture stand for a while. Warm milk, do not boil, beat the eggs and egg yolk together, gradually add the sugar and a little of the hot milk. Mix well, add remaining milk and vanilla essence. Spread the glacé fruit mixture over base of flan case, pour over beaten eggs and milk, sprinkle with grated nutmeg. Bake at Mark 6, in the centre of the oven, until the egg custard is set, about 35 – 40 mins. Decorate with glacé cherries. **Serves 6**

Spiced Apple Pudding

A delicious hot pudding for autumn days. Ideal for using windfall apples.

Base	Filling
4 oz wholemeal bread	1½ lb cooking apples
2 oz soft brown sugar	3 oz raisins
1 oz butter	1 teasp. apple pie spice
Topping	½ pt water
3 oz demerara sugar	3 oz soft brown sugar
3 oz quick cooking oats	pinch of salt
3 oz melted butter	

Peel, core and slice apples; if using windfalls, these can be half eating and half cooking varieties. Stew for 10 mins, with the raisins, water, sugar, salt and spice (cinnamon and nutmeg mixed can replace apple pie spice). Crumble bread and mix with sugar, place in base of deep ovenproof dish, dot with small pieces of butter. Pour over cooked apples. Mix oats, sugar and melted butter, scatter over apples. Bake at Mark 5 for 25 mins until crisp and golden. Serve with cream. **Serves 6 – 8**

Mincemeat and Cherry Layer

1 small (8 oz) can cherries	2 eggs
8 oz mincemeat	4 oz S.R. flour
4 oz margarine	2 oz fresh white breadcrumbs
4 oz caster sugar	2 tablesps milk

Drain cherries and mix 2 tablesps of juice into mincemeat. Cream margarine and caster sugar together until light and fluffy. Beat eggs in separately. Fold in sifted flour and breadcrumbs. Mix to a soft dropping consistency with milk. Place cherries in bottom of greased basin, then fill with alternate layers of sponge mixture and mincemeat, ending with sponge layer. Bake on centre shelf of oven for 45 mins at Mark 4. Turn on to a hot dish and serve with custard or cream. **Serves 4 – 6**

Peeping Peaches

1×15 oz can peach halves	1×7½ oz pkt frozen puff pastry
3 glacé cherries	beaten egg to glaze apricot jam

Roll out pastry into 2 oblongs each 12″×6″. Drain peaches and cut cherries in half.

Arrange six peaches, cut side downwards, along one half of pastry to within ½ inch of edges. Dampen edges and place the other half on top sealing edges well.

Roll out pastry trimmings into three strips. Dampen and place 1 strip lengthwise and 2 strips across the pastry, dividing peaches into squares.

Place on a dampened baking sheet. Using scissors, make a hole in the pastry on the top of each peach with 8 small cuts outward in a star shape. Brush with beaten egg and then fold back pastry points to expose each peach.

Bake at Mark 7 for 20 mins. When cooked and golden brown brush peaches with apricot jam and place ½ cherry in the centre of each. **Serves 6**

Mincemeat and Apple Macaroon Flan

1×8 inch baked shortcrust pastry flan case
2 tablesps mincemeat
½ pt apple purée
2 egg whites
2 oz caster sugar
2 oz ground almonds
1 oz almonds, finely chopped

Spread mincemeat in base of the flan case. Cover with apple purée. Whisk egg whites until stiff and standing in peaks. Add the sugar gradually whisking well with each addition.

Fold in ground almonds using a metal spoon. Pile the mixture on top of apples, sprinkle with almonds. Bake at Mark 4 for 30 mins. **Serves 6–8**

Farmhouse Cheesecake

7-8 inch square cooked flan case	¼ pt double cream beaten
8 oz cottage cheese – sieved	2 egg whites beaten
2 egg yolks	Rind and juice of ½ lemon
2 oz caster sugar	*To decorate* mandarin oranges and black grapes

Place sieved cheese, egg yolks, sugar and lemon juice and rind in a bowl and mix together. Fold in beaten cream and egg whites. Pour into pastry case. Place in centre of oven, at Mark 5 for 30–35 mins. Serve hot or cold, decorated with mandarin oranges and black grapes. **Serves 6–8**

Rhubarb and Ginger Meringue Pie

7-8 inch cooked flan case	
1 lb rhubarb	1 level teasp. ground ginger
4 tablesps water	1 oz preserved ginger pieces
3 oz sugar	1 heaped teasp. arrowroot
Topping	
2 egg whites	4 oz caster sugar

Wash and cut rhubarb into 1 inch lengths; poach in water with sugar, ground ginger and chopped ginger pieces for 5 mins. Strain, blend arrowroot with juice and cook for 1–2 mins, stirring until thickened. Place fruit in flan case and pour over arrowroot sauce. Beat egg whites until stiff, beat in half the sugar, then fold in remaining sugar, pipe on top of flan. Bake for 20–30 mins at Mark 2. **Serves 6–8**

Banana Twists

4 small bananas	
juice of $\frac{1}{2}$ a lemon	
$\frac{1}{2}$ lb puff pastry	
caster sugar	

Roll the pastry into a long strip $\frac{1}{4}$ inch thick and cut into strips 1 inch wide. Brush the pastry with lemon juice and twist the pastry round the bananas, overlapping slightly. Brush the tops with water and sprinkle on some caster sugar. Bake at Mark 7 for 15 mins. Serve hot or cold with fresh cream.
Serves 4

Lemon Tassie

4 eggs	juice & rind of 4 lemons
$\frac{3}{4}$ teasp. cream of tartar	1 pt cream
$9\frac{1}{2}$ oz caster sugar	crystallized fruit

Separate eggs. Beat whites with cream of tartar until stiff, gradually fold in 8 oz caster sugar. Pipe mixture in the form of 3 inch nests, on to an oiled baking sheet. Bake at Mark $\frac{1}{4}$ for 2 hours.

Beat egg yolks with lemon juice, rind and remaining sugar. Cook over hot water until thick. Do not allow to boil. Remove from heat, allow to cool until almost set, beat half of cream until fluffy, fold into lemon mixture. Chill. Whip remaining cream sweeten with caster or icing sugar. Fill meringue nests with lemon mixture decorate with cream and crystallized fruit. **Serves 4–6**

Autumn Glory

2 pkts boudoir biscuits	1 tablesp. milk
$\frac{1}{2}$ lb brambles	1 tablesp. lemon juice
$\frac{1}{2}$ lb cooking apples	1 green eating apple
1 apple & bramble jelly	small carton double cream

Line base and sides of a 6 inch soufflé dish with the boudoir biscuits. Reserve 6 brambles and place washed remainder in a pan with the peeled and sliced cooking apples. Cook till thick and pulpy, approx 10–15 mins, then sieve into a bowl. Return purée to pan and add the jelly cubes. When jelly melts pour into a measuring jug and make up to 1 pt with cold water, and pour into lined dish. Refrigerate till set. Invert soufflé dish on to serving plate. Whip double cream and milk till thick, place in piping bag with star pipe and decorate top and sides.

Thinly slice green apple without peeling, dip in lemon juice and arrange on top with reserved brambles. **Serves 4–6**

Lemon Coltart

$4\frac{1}{2}$ oz butter	3 lemons
9 oz digestive biscuits (crushed)	9 oz cream cheese
$1\frac{1}{2}$ lemon jellies	12 oz caster sugar
9 fluid oz water	$\frac{3}{4}$ tin of evaporated milk (chilled)

Decorate with double cream (whipped), lemon slices

Melt butter in pan and stir in crushed digestive biscuits. Press mixture into a loose-bottomed 8–9 inch cake tin, to cover the base and half way up the sides.

Dissolve the jelly in measured hot water, allow to cool, squeeze lemons. Cream together cheese and sugar until light and fluffy; beat in lemon juice and lemon jelly. Whisk chilled evaporated milk until it thickens, fold into cheese mixture. Pour into biscuit lined tin. Chill in refrigerator, for at least 4 hours or preferably overnight. Remove from tin, decorate with piped cream and lemon slices; serve.

If a smaller quantity is required reduce ingredients by one third, using a small tin of evaporated milk and a 7 inch cake tin. **Serves 6–8**

Lady's Secret

4 oz vanilla wafers	6 tablesps melted butter
1 egg	2 oz nuts, roasted and chopped
1 egg yolk	$\frac{1}{4}$ pt double cream, whipped
8 oz caster sugar	wafers to decorate
3 oz cocoa	

Crumble the wafers coarsely. Beat the eggs and sugar together until smooth, add the cocoa and mix well, stir in the melted butter, nuts and wafers. Put the mixture into a greased and lined tin, chill in the refrigerator for at least 2 hours. When ready to serve, decorate with cream and wafers. **Serves 3**

Iced Pineapple Liqueur

1 medium pineapple	sugar to dredge
$\frac{1}{4}$ pt water	8 oz caster sugar
rind and juice of 1 lemon	2 tablesps maraschino liqueur
10 maraschino cherries	

Split the pineapple down the centre, scrape the flesh and juice into a bowl. Discard the centre core. Sprinkle the shell of the pineapple with sugar and chill.

Make a purée of the flesh and juice in a blender, add water, sugar, lemon rind and juice, place in a pan and boil for 5 mins, cool then turn into a freezing tray. Freeze until mushy. Put frozen pineapple, liqueur and cherries into a bowl and beat well. Return mixture to freezing tray and freeze until firm. To serve, scoop pineapple ice out of tray and pile into the chilled shell. Decorate with cherries and place on a bed of crushed ice. **Serves 4**

Chocolate Surprise

$\frac{1}{2}$ pt double cream, stiffly beaten	2×6 inch chocolate sponge cakes
5 oz icing sugar	1 tablesp. brandy
1 oz hazelnuts, toasted and chopped	1 tablesp. Cointreau
4 oz cherries, stoned	1 bunch of cherries
2 oz dark chocolate, grated	

Combine cream and sugar and add nuts, cherries and chocolate, and chill in refrigerator. Mix together brandy and liqueur. Line a pudding basin with two crossed strips of greaseproof paper then with triangles of sponge, cut into four and then horizontally. Sprinkle the liqueurs over the sponge. Spoon in the cream mixture and cover with sponge. Chill for at least 2 hours before serving. Loosen with a knife and turn on to a plate. Decorate with a bunch of cherries and a sprinkling of icing sugar. **Serves 6**

White Bonnets and Highland Cream

1 lb stoned fruit	2 oz sugar
$\frac{1}{4}$ pt wine	

See that all fruit is quite sound. Slit with a silver knife then remove and discard stones, though half-a-dozen can be cracked and the kernels added to the fruit if liked. Pour wine into a small shallow saucepan. Add sugar. Stir till dissolved, then add fruit. Cover pan closely. Simmer very gently for 10 mins. Cool slightly. Turn carefully into basin. When chilled spoon into individual glasses. Top each with Highland Cream. **Serves 6–7**

N.B. This can be made with damsons, red wine and brown sugar or greengages, white wine and granulated sugar.

Highland Cream

2 egg yolks	2 egg whites
6 oz caster sugar	4 tablesps malt whisky or Drambuie
1 teasp. lemon juice	

Beat egg yolks and 4 oz sugar in a bowl over hot water till thick and creamy. Beat in whisky and juice. Cool slightly. Whisk whites until stiff, gradually add remaining 2 oz sugar to yolk mixture. Fold yolk mixture into whites until well blended. Serve at once (or chill for 2–3 hours and serve). This recipe makes 1 pt.

Banana and Orange Meringue

2 oz brown sugar	2 egg whites
5 ripe bananas	1 oz caster sugar
2 oranges	whipped cream
1 tablesp. lemon juice	
2 egg whites	
1 oz caster sugar	
whipped cream	

Sprinkle 1 oz brown sugar evenly over the bottom of a shallow pie dish. Peel bananas and cut in half lengthwise and then across. Arrange on top of sugar with the finely grated rind of one orange. Remove peel and pith from both oranges and slice thinly, lay these on top of bananas. Put remaining brown sugar on top and sprinkle with lemon juice. Beat egg whites, add caster sugar a little at a time and continue beating until stiff. Pile on top of fruit. Bake at Mark 4 for 15 mins, allow to cool, serve chilled with whipped cream. **Serves 4**

Prune and Apricot Ginger Compote

| 8 dried apricots | 2 small oranges |
| 6 dried prunes | 2 tablesps syrup from a jar of preserved ginger |

Remove prune stones. Place prunes in a bowl with apricots, add the finely grated rind of one orange, then the juice from both oranges. Add sufficient warm water to cover fruit. Stir in the ginger syrup, cover, and leave to soak overnight.

Turn contents of bowl into a pan, cover and simmer gently for 10 mins. Allow to cool, place in serving dish. Chill. **Serves 2**

Glenfiddich Chocolate Mousse

6 oz sweet chocolate	5 eggs, separated
1 teasp. vanilla extract	1 teasp. instant coffee
½ pt double cream	2 tablesps Glenfiddich whisky

Melt the chocolate in a bowl over hot water. Remove from the heat and allow to cool. Lightly beat the egg yolks and stir them gradually into the melted chocolate. Flavour to taste with vanilla and instant coffee diluted in a little hot water. Beat the cream until thick, stir in the whisky and fold into the chocolate mixture. Beat the egg whites until stiff and fold into the mixture a little at a time. Pour into a serving dish or individual glasses. Chill for at least 2 hours or overnight. Decorate with cream and serve. **Serves 6–8**

Raspberry Syllabub

½ lb raspberries	2 dessertsps rose water *or*
2 oz sugar	2 teasps lemon juice
½ pt double cream	7½ fluid oz sweet white wine

Set aside half the raspberries. Bruise the remainder lightly with a wooden spoon and sprinkle them with the rose water or lemon juice and half the sugar. Whisk the cream until it is quite stiff. Gradually pour the rest of the sugar and the white wine into the cream, beating continuously so that it stands up in soft peaks. Stir two tablesps of this mixture into the bruised raspberries, then fold this gently into the remainder of the cream. (The effect should be as if the cream had been lightly marbled with pale pink.) Finally, stir in the whole raspberries, spoon the mixture into individual bowls or glasses and chill lightly. Serve with macaroons or sponge fingers. **Serves 4 – 6**

Praline Cream

¾ pt milk	¼ lb praline, crushed
3 egg yolks	3-4 macaroons, crushed
1½ oz caster sugar	1 teasp. rum
½ oz gelatine	3-4 oz chocolate
3-4 tablesps water	½ pt double cream
1 egg white	1-2 tablesps red currant jelly
6 small paper cornets of greaseproof paper	¾ pt double cream for decoration, thickly whipped

Scald the milk and beat the egg yolks with the caster sugar till light. Pour on the milk and blend, then return to the pan and thicken over a moderate heat without boiling. Strain and cool. Dissolve gelatine in the water and add to the custard. When cool and nearly set, fold in whipped cream and stiffly beaten egg white. Add the praline and pour half the mixture into a lightly oiled 7 inch round tin. Quickly sprinkle on the crushed macaroons and rum and pour in the remaining custard and leave to set. Meanwhile melt the chocolate and line the paper cornets with it. Leave to set then peel off the paper. Turn out the custard and thickly coat in stiffly whipped cream. Stir the red currant jelly till smooth and pipe lines across the top of the custard at 1 inch intervals. Then with the point of a knife draw lines across the jelly at 1 inch intervals then repeat in the opposite direction between each line, to give a feathered effect. Fill the point of each cornet with a little red currant jelly then fill with cream and arrange on top. **Serves 6**

Cherry and Almond Flan

4 oz sweet shortcrust pastry	4 oz ground almonds
1 tin cherry pie filling	4 oz icing sugar
3 egg whites	1 teasp. almond essence

Line 7 inch flan ring with shortcrust pastry and bake 'blind' at Mark 6 for 20 mins. When cool, half fill with cherries. Lightly whisk egg whites and essence, combine with mixed ground almonds and icing sugar. Pour over fruit and bake at Mark 5 till brown, approx. 30 mins. **Serves 4 – 6**

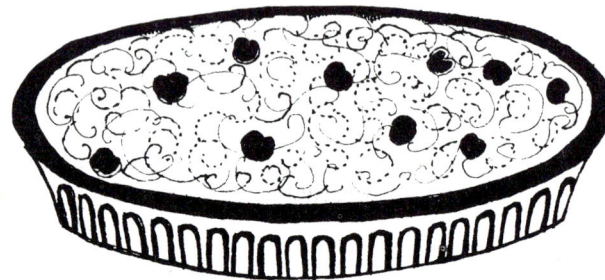

Apple & Hazelnut Galette

	For Filling
3 oz hazelnuts (shelled)	1 lb dessert apples (pippin variety)
3 oz butter	1 tablesp. smooth apricot jam
2 rounded tablesps caster sugar	grated rind of 1 lemon
4½ oz plain flour	1 tablesp. orange peel (finely chopped)
pinch of salt	2 tablesps sultanas
	2 tablesps currants
	icing sugar (for dusting)
	whipped cream (optional)

Brown the shelled nuts in the oven at Mark 4 until husks can be rubbed off (about 7–8 mins when nuts should be a deep golden-brown). Reserve a few whole nuts for decoration and pass remainder through a small cheese grater or mincer, or work until fine in a blender.

Soften the butter, add sugar and beat together until light and fluffy. Sift the flour with a pinch of salt and stir into the mixture with the prepared nuts. Chill for at least 30 mins.

Meanwhile prepare filling. Peel, core and slice the apples. Put them in a pan with apricot jam and grated lemon rind. Cook over slow heat until soft, then add orange peel, sultanas and currants; simmer for another 5 mins.

Divide the pastry mixture in two and place each piece on a lightly-floured baking sheet. Roll or pat into very thin rounds 9 inches in diameter. Bake for about 10 mins in the oven at Mark 5. Do not let pastry brown or it will taste scorched. While still warm and on the baking sheet, trim edges and cut one round into eight portions, then slide carefully on to a wire rack to cool.

Cover the whole round of pastry with apple mixture, spread evenly and place the cut portions on top. Dust with icing sugar. Serve with whipped cream, or pipe rosettes of cream on each portion and decorate with whole hazelnuts. **Serves 6–8**

Profiteroles au Crème de Menthe

	Icing
6 oz butter	1 egg white
1 pt water	4–6 oz icing sugar
10 oz plain flour	Crème de Menthe to flavour
8 standard eggs	
½ pt whipped cream	

Melt butter in the water and bring to boil. Remove from the heat and quickly add the flour all at once. Beat until the paste is smooth and forms a ball in the centre of the pan. Allow to cool slightly, then beat in eggs gradually, adding just enough to give a smooth mixture of piping consistency.

Using large plain nozzle, pipe on to prepared baking sheets small dots of paste. Cook at Mark 7 for about 20–25 mins. Allow to cool. Make small hole to let steam escape. Fill with cream, pile up on serving dish. Drizzle over with Crème de Menthe icing. **Serves 6–8**

Whisky Biscuit Cake

2 oz walnuts	2 tablesps Scotch whisky
4 oz digestive biscuits	8 oz unsalted butter melted
4 oz tea biscuits	8 oz plain chocolate, melted
1 oz caster sugar	2 eggs

Chop nuts roughly and break biscuits into small pieces. Beat eggs and sugar till thick and creamy. Gradually add melted butter beating all the time. Beat in melted chocolate gradually. Fold in biscuits, nuts and whisky. Spread in well oiled 7 inch tin with a loose base. Chill. Remove from tin and serve at room temperature. Serve alone or with cream or ice-cream. **Serves 8**

Cherry Cheese Cake

2 pkts sponge fingers	½ pt double cream
4 oz butter	1 tin cherry pie filling
12 oz cream cheese	4 oz caster sugar

Crush the sponge fingers into crumbs with a rolling pin. Melt the butter and stir in the crumbs. Press into a greased 8–9 inch flan tin. Chill.

Beat the cream cheese and sugar together. Lightly whip the cream and fold into the cheese. Turn into the flan tin and chill. Just before serving remove from tin and pour over pie filling. **Serves 6–8**

Chocolate & Raspberry Gâteau

3 eggs	sweet white wine (to flavour)
4½ oz caster sugar	raspberry liqueur (to flavour)
3 oz plain flour	½ lb raspberries
pinch salt	caster sugar
1 tablesp. boiling water	double cream
3 oz plain chocolate	

Separate the eggs. Beat the egg yolks, boiling water and 2½ oz caster sugar in a bowl over hot water till thick and creamy. Then remove from the heat. Whisk the whites stiffly then whisk in sugar. Fold this into the yolk mixture with the flour and salt. Turn into greased and floured 8 inch square tin. Bake at Mark 4 for 25 mins. Turn out and cool. Meanwhile, melt the chocolate carefully and spread evenly and moderately thickly over a large square of greased or wax paper, and when just set, mark into 2 inch squares. Leave in a cool place to harden completely. Sugar the fruit and leave for a short while. Sprinkle the cake with the wine and liqueur. Spread the cream on the sides of the cake and press the chocolate squares round the sides of the cake slightly overlapping. They will rise above the top of the cake. Fill the cake with the fruit and decorate with more cream. **Serves 6–8**

Sherry Gâteau

2 thin 8–10 inch sponge cakes
2 eggs, separated
4 tablesps caster sugar
½ oz (1 envelope) powdered gelatine dissolved in 3 tablesps water
1×6 oz can cream, chilled
4 fluid oz sherry
grated chocolate ⎱ for decoration glace cherries ⎰

Place one layer of sponge on a plate and secure a double band of greaseproof paper, 5 inches deep, around to form a collar.

Beat the egg yolks and sugar until light and foamy. Mix in the sherry and dissolved gelatine and put aside until mixture begins to set. Whisk the cream. When sherry mixture begins to thicken, whisk the egg whites stiffly and fold into the sherry mixture with ¾ of the cream. Pour the mixture over the sponge and place the second layer lightly on top.

Spread remaining cream on top of gâteau and decorate with the chocolate and cherries. Refrigerate for at least one hour or preferably overnight. Remove greaseproof collar carefully before serving. **Serves 8–10**

T/E/A/T/I/M/E T/R/E/A/T/S

In our busy lives today, there's little time for the old tradition of Afternoon Tea. But being Scottish Home Economists, we feel that baking is a tradition which is still very much a part of the Scottish way of life. Our reputation for hospitality is not unfounded, as any guest, neighbour or friend will be invited to have a cup of tea or coffee within minutes of entering the door. How satisfying to be able to offer fruit loaf, buns or biscuits to accompany a refreshing beverage!

The problem is finding the time to bake, so the teatime treats we offer are fruit-breads, scones and traybakes, which can be quickly prepared, and cut up to provide ample for a number of 'cups of tea'. The last few recipes are for decorated gâteaux for special occasions.

Quick Brown Bread

8 oz wholemeal flour	½ teasp. salt
4 oz S.R. flour	golden syrup
1 teasp. bicarbonate soda	milk as required (approx. ½ pt)
1 teasp. cream of tartar	

Place dry ingredients in a bowl. Stir in enough syrup to fold round the knife and add enough milk to form a soft dough. Place the dough in a well-greased loaf tin and cover with foil. Bake at Mark 4 for 50 mins. Remove foil and bake for another 10 mins.

Very quick – reliable and easy to make.

Irish Tea Bread

6 tablesps strong tea	1 oz margarine (melted)
½ lb mixed fruit	4½ oz plain flour
3 oz soft brown sugar	¼ level teasp. bicarbonate of soda
1 small egg, lightly beaten	

Place the tea, mixed fruit and sugar in bowl, cover and leave overnight. Stir in egg and melted margarine. Fold in flour and bicarbonate of soda. Place mixture in 1 lb loaf tin, previously bottom-lined with greaseproof paper and brushed with melted margarine. Smooth the top. Bake on middle shelf at Mark 4 for one hour. Turn out. Dredge with icing sugar, serve sliced and spread with butter.

Banana Bread

2 oz butter or margarine	1 egg
3 oz molasses sugar	3 tablesps milk
1 banana	5 oz S.R. flour
1 level teasp. cinnamon	icing sugar and cherries

Cream butter and sugar till light and fluffy, mash banana and beat into creamed mixture. Add beaten egg using a little flour if necessary. Add milk and fold in sieved flour and cinnamon. Bake in a greased 1 lb loaf tin at Mark 3 for 40–45 mins. To decorate make a thin glacé icing and pour over cake with a row of cherries down the centre.

Malty Fruit Loaf

7 oz sultanas	1 egg
2 rounded tablesps malted bedtime drink	4 oz S.R. flour
¼ pt boiling water	4 oz wheatmeal flour
4 oz granulated sugar	½ level teasp. salt

Mix together sultanas, malted drink, boiling water and sugar, cover and leave to soak overnight or for at least 4 hours. Grease and line the base of a 1 lb loaf tin. Stir egg, flour and salt into fruit mixture and mix well. Place in the tin and bake at Mark 3 for 1½ hours. Leave in tin for 5 mins before turning out. Serve sliced with butter. This loaf improves with keeping.

Apricot Bran Loaf

2 oz 'All Bran'	¼ pt milk
4 oz sugar	4 oz S.R. flour
6 oz dried apricots (chopped)	

Place 'All Bran', sugar and apricots into a bowl, stir in the milk and set aside for 1 hour. Fold in sieved flour. Pour into a greased 1 lb loaf tin. Bake at Mark 4 for 1½ hours. Remove from tin and allow to cool.

Serve sliced, spread with butter. Best eaten when freshly baked.

Zucchini Bread

3 eggs (lightly beaten)	¼ teasp. baking powder
¼ pt vegetable oil	2 teasps bicarbonate of soda
8 oz caster sugar	3 teasps cinnamon
8 oz courgettes	1 teasp. salt
1 teasp. vanilla essence	6 oz raisins
8 oz plain flour	6 oz nuts (chopped)

Add the oil, vanilla essence, sugar and courgettes, coarsely grated, to beaten eggs. Sift together flour, baking powder, bicarbonate of soda, cinnamon and salt. Stir into egg mixture. Add raisins and chopped nuts. Place the mixture in two greased 1 lb loaf tins. Bake at Mark 4 for 1 hour.

Butterscotch Scones

7 oz flour	pinch of salt
1 oz cornflour	1 oz butter
1 teasp. baking powder	milk to mix
Filling **butter and brown sugar**	

Sift the flour, cornflour, baking powder and salt together. Rub in the butter, and mix to an elastic dough with the milk. Knead lightly on a floured board and roll out into an oblong shape ¼ inch thick, spread with the butter and sprinkle well with soft brown sugar. Roll up like a Swiss roll. Cut into slices and bake at Mark 7 for 8–10 mins.

Pancakes

½ lb flour (sifted)	½ teasp. cream of tartar
½ teasp. salt	1 beaten egg
1 oz caster sugar	approx. 8 fl oz buttermilk
½ teasp. bicarbonate of soda	

Heat girdle. Mix the dry ingredients in a basin. Make a well in the centre and add the egg and about half the milk. Stir until thick, then add rest of milk until the consistency of thick cream is reached. Pour into a jug. Rub girdle with lard and pour batter out into rounds about 3 inch across. Cook until light brown below and bubbles form on top, then turn and cook on the other side. Serve hot, or cold with butter and jam.

Treacle Scones

½ lb flour	½ teasp. mixed spice
½ teasp. baking soda	1 oz margarine
1 teasp. cream of tartar	1 oz caster sugar
½ teasp. salt	1 tablesp. treacle
½ teasp. ground cinnamon	milk to mix

Sieve dry ingredients and rub in the margarine. Add the sugar. Dilute the treacle with a little milk and mix to a light dough adding more milk as necessary. Turn on to a floured board. Knead lightly, roll out and cut into scones. Bake on a greased tray at Mark 8 for 15 mins.

Ginger Shortcake

	Icing
3 oz margarine	**4 heaped tablesps icing sugar**
2 oz sugar	**4 oz margarine**
6 oz plain flour	**2 teasps syrup**
1 teasp. ginger	*Decoration* 1 oz preserved ginger, chopped

Cream margarine and sugar, add flour and ginger. Spread into a greased Swiss roll tin and bake at Mark 5 for 20 to 30 mins.

Place icing ingredients in a pan and heat slowly until blended. Ice when hot and cut into fingers when cool. Decorate with preserved ginger.

Mincemeat Cookies

¼ lb mincemeat	**¼ lb flour**
¼ teasp. salt	**½ teasp. baking powder**
1 oz margarine or lard	**1 oz brown sugar**

Sift flour, salt and baking powder together. Cream fat and sugar, add egg and beat well. Stir in dry ingredients and then mincemeat. Form into a roll 3 inch in diameter, wrap in waxed paper and chill overnight in the refrigerator. Next day slice ⅛ inch thick and bake on a greased baking tin at Mark 4 for about 10 mins until golden brown.

Fruit Shorties

Filling	*Crumble*
2-3 oz chopped dates	**4 oz plain flour**
6 oz mixed dried fruit	**4 oz semolina**
1 med. cooking apple	**4 oz margarine**
3 tablesps lemon juice and	**3 oz caster sugar**
3 tablesps water	**a little granulated sugar**
7″×9″ baking tin	

Place fruit, dates and chopped apple into saucepan. Add juice and water. Cook, stirring occasionally until soft and pulpy. Place flour and semolina in a bowl. Rub in margarine, add caster sugar. Press half of crumble evenly into tin, spread with fruit filling and cover with remaining crumble, pressing down lightly. Bake in centre of oven, Mark 5, for 35 mins. Leave in tin till cold. Cut into squares or triangles.

Chinese Chews

½ lb chopped dates	3 oz plain flour
4 oz chopped walnuts	1 teasp. baking powder
7 oz soft brown sugar	3 eggs

Mix dry ingredients together and add 3 lightly beaten eggs. Pour into greased, lined Swiss roll tin. Bake for 25–30 mins at Mark 4. Allow to cool. Mark into fingers or squares. Cut when cold.

Dark Sticky Gingerbread

2 oz golden syrup	2 oz caster sugar
6 oz treacle	1 teasp. bicarbonate of soda
4 oz margarine	1 teasp. mixed spice
¼ pt milk	2 teasps ginger
2 eggs	½ teasp. cinnamon
8 oz plain flour	

Dissolve bicarbonate of soda in a little of measured milk. Melt margarine, sugar, syrup and treacle in a medium-sized pan, stir in beaten eggs, dissolved bicarbonate of soda and remainder of milk. Fold in sieved dry ingredients; pour into greased, lined, 8 inch square tin approximately 2 inches deep. Bake at Mark 3 for 45 mins – 1 hour. Allow to cool for 10–15 mins before turning out onto cooling tray.

N.B. 3 oz dried fruit may be added with dry ingredients if desired.

Paradise Slice

8 oz shortcrust pastry	2 oz S.R. flour
4 oz margarine	jam
4 oz caster sugar	1 oz sultanas
2 eggs	1 oz currants
2 oz ground almonds	1 oz chopped cherries

Line a Swiss roll tin with shortcrust pastry, prick with a fork. Line with greaseproof paper, cover with baking beans, bake at Mark 6 for 15 to 20 mins. Remove beans and paper, spread base with jam. Cream margarine and sugar, add beaten eggs, fold in flour and ground almonds. Sprinkle mixed dried fruit over pastry. Spread sponge mixture on top, bake at Mark 4 for 25–30 mins. Remove from oven, dredge with caster sugar. Cut into slices when cold.

Peppermint Crunch

½ lb tea biscuits (crushed)	3 oz caster sugar
2 tablesps drinking chocolate	1 egg
3½ oz margarine	
Icing	
¾ lb icing sugar	peppermint essence
6 oz plain cooking chocolate	green colouring

Melt margarine, sugar and drinking chocolate in a pan, add crushed biscuits and well beaten egg. Spread over the base of a 7″×10″ Swiss roll tin. Leave overnight to set. Mix icing sugar with very little hot water. It should be very stiff. Add peppermint essence and colouring. Spread on top of biscuit mixture. When set, coat with chocolate, melted in a bowl over hot water. Cut the crunch into fingers.

Bridal Slices

8 oz shortcrust pastry	4 oz cherries
2 eggs	2 oz margarine
8 oz currants	1 teasp. mixed spice
4 oz caster sugar	8 oz marzipan
6 tablesps crushed granola biscuits	icing

Grease Swiss roll tin. Line with pastry. Cream butter, sugar and add beaten eggs. Mix well. Add crushed biscuits, spice and fruit. Spread over pastry and cook for 45 mins at Mark 4. Cool. Brush with jam, cover with marzipan and Royal icing or hot water icing. A useful recipe to make during the festive season. Left-over icing from the Christmas cake would give a perfect finish. When icing is almost dry, cut into slices.

Raisin Rhapsody

3 oz caster sugar	1 egg
8 oz mixed dried fruit	2 oz melted margarine
2 tablesps S.R. flour	few cherries (chopped)
6 oz shortcrust pastry	6 oz icing sugar
raspberry jam	2 oz coconut
Decoration cherries and angelica if desired	

Line Swiss roll tin with pastry, spread raspberry jam sparingly over the base of tin.

Beat egg, stir into other ingredients. Spread mixture over pastry. Bake at Mark 4 for 30 mins (centre oven). When cold, mix icing sugar with a little hot water, coat top of raisin rhapsody and immediately sprinkle over the dessicated coconut. Cut into fingers or squares. For a final touch each piece can be decorated with tiny pieces of cherry and angelica before sprinkling over coconut.

Banana Pastry Puff

7½ oz packet frozen puff pastry, thawed	2 oz raisins
	1 oz plain biscuits
1 medium-size banana	1 tablesp. granulated sugar
½ lb cooking apples	1 small egg white, lightly beaten
rind and juice of half medium-size lemon	

Roll out the pastry. Cut out a 9 inch round and an 8 inch round. Put the 8 inch round on the baking sheet, prick all over with a fork. Mash the banana and mix with peeled and chopped apple. Now mix in lemon juice, rind, raisins, finely crushed biscuits and 1 level dessertsp. sugar. Spoon this onto the pastry, leaving ½ inch clear all the way round. Brush edge with a little egg white. Put the other round of pastry on top; press edges to seal. Brush top with egg white and mark a lattice pattern with a knife. Sprinkle a dessertsp. of sugar on top. Bake at Mark 7 for 30 mins.

Bush Babies

Sufficient shortcrust pastry to line 12 patty tins.

1 oz margarine	1 egg
1 oz sugar	2 oz dried fruit
1 dessertsp. golden syrup	vanilla essence

Cream margarine and sugar, beat in syrup then the whisked egg and finally fruit and essence. Mix well and divide into pastry cases. Bake 15 mins at Mark 5.

Coconut Macaroons

Like the previous recipe, this is designed for combining left-over shortcrust pastry and store cupboard ingredients, to provide a simple teatime fancy.

Sufficient pastry to line 12 tartlet or patty tins.

1 egg	4 oz dessicated coconut
4 oz caster sugar	lemon curd

Place ¼ teasp. of lemon curd in the base of each pastry tartlet. Whisk egg and sugar until a thick cream is obtained. Fold in coconut and spoon the mixture on top of lemon curd. Each tartlet should only be two-thirds full, to allow for rising during cooking. Bake at Mark 4 until pale golden brown. Allow to cool slightly then remove from tins and cool on wire tray.

Celebration Ring

½ lb flaky pastry	2 oz chopped nuts
½ lb marzipan	1 oz chopped peel
2 oz glacé cherries	2 tablesps sherry
1 oz angelica	¼ teasp. almond essence

Optional Meringue

2 egg whites	
4 oz caster sugar	Make into meringue mix by usual method

Decoration 2 or 3 glacé cherries and angelica.

Soak fruit, nuts, sherry and almond essence overnight. Roll out pastry into an oblong. Roll out marzipan and cover with fruit mixture. Roll this up like a Swiss roll. Now place the marzipan on top of pastry oblong, wrap the pastry firmly round marzipan. Place on lightly greased baking sheet, forming into a circle or horseshoe shape. Bake at Mark 6 for 30–35 mins. The celebration ring may be brushed with a little water icing and decorated with cherries and angelica or coated with meringue mixture, which should be roughly forked or peaked. Place back in the oven at Mark 4 and allow to brown lightly for 10–15 mins. Cool and serve decorated with glacé fruits.

Sachertorte

8 oz plain chocolate	*Icing*
4 oz unsalted butter	5 oz chocolate
6½ oz sugar	2½ oz butter
6 eggs	*Decoration*
3 oz ground almonds or other nuts	Butter icing or double cream
1½ oz S.R. flour	Cherries

Melt the chocolate over a low heat; when it is soft, cream it with the butter, sugar and egg yolks. Fold in the stiffly beaten egg whites, almonds and flour. Put in a greased and lined 9 inch cake tin and bake in a moderate oven, Mark 4, for at least 45 mins. This cake should remain slightly moist in the centre.

Icing

Melt the chocolate over a low heat. Mix it with the melted butter, leave for 20–30 mins to cool to a coating consistency and pour over the cake. Decorate with butter icing or whipped cream and cherries.

Christmas Crown

8 oz butter	4 oz S.R. flour, sifted
8 oz caster sugar	3 oz halved glacé cherries
4 eggs	3 oz glacé pineapple
4 oz ground almonds	3 oz citron peel
9 inch ring-mould (3 pt capacity)	3 oz ginger pieces

Orange Frosting	*Decoration*
12 oz granulated sugar	glacé cherries
4 tablesps orange juice	Angelica
2 egg whites	lemon and orange slices
¼ level teasp. cream of tartar	

Grease ring-mould with melted lard, dredge with flour and shake out surplus.

Chop the crystallised pineapple, peel and ginger pieces finely. Wash and dry cherries.

Cream butter and sugar, beat eggs and gradually add them to the cream mixture, beating well after each addition. Stir in ground almonds and sifted flour. Fold in chopped fruit. Turn mixture into ring-mould. Bake at Mark 4 for about 1 hour, allow cake to shrink slightly then turn out onto a cooling tray.

Mix egg whites, granulated sugar, cream of tartar and orange juice in a bowl over a pan of boiling water. Stir gently, until sugar dissolves then beat with a rotary beater until thick. The mixture should leave an obvious trail when the whisk is lifted from the bowl. Remove from heat and continue beating until the mixture cools slightly. Spread quickly over cake leaving a rough peaked surface. Before the icing sets completely decorate with half cherries, diamonds of angelica and small pieces of orange and lemon slices.

Sunshine Gâteau

Sponge	*Meringues*
3 oz caster sugar	1 egg white
3 eggs, beaten	2 oz caster sugar
3 oz plain flour (sieved)	*Filling and Decoration*
1 oz melted margarine	½ pt double cream
	1 small pineapple *or*
	tin of pineapple rings
	fresh or tinned red cherries

Put 3 oz caster sugar and 3 eggs into a bowl over a pan of hot water, whisk until light and creamy and the mixture thickens. Remove from hot water, continue whisking until the contents of the bowl cool. Lightly fold in flour and melted margarine, pour into a greased and floured 8 inch sandwich tin. Bake in the centre of the oven at Mark 4 for 30–35 mins. Cool on wire tray.

Make meringues by whisking one egg white until stiff, add half the caster sugar, whisk again, then fold in remaining caster sugar. Pipe small meringues on to a baking tray covered with oiled greaseproof paper. Bake at Mark ½ until dry and crisp.

To complete the gâteau, whisk double cream until stiff. Cut sponge through the centre, sandwich the two rounds together with some of the whipped cream. Spread remainder of cream round sides and on top. Press small meringues round sides of cake. Peel and slice fresh pineapple or drain tinned pineapple. Arrange 6 slices on top of cake, place a cherry (stoned), in the centre of each pineapple ring and a few in the centre of the gâteau. Keep in refrigerator until ready to serve.

Golden Gâteau

	Filling
3 small oranges	*Filling*
Cake	**orange liqueur**
8 oz soft margarine	**½ pt double cream**
8 oz caster sugar	**½ tin mandarin oranges (drained)**
4 standard eggs	*Decoration*
8 oz S.R. flour	**3 oz flaked almonds**
	Butter Icing
	12 oz icing sugar
	6 oz butter

Wash oranges, and cut four thin slices from the centre of one orange and three slices from the centre of another orange. Reserve for decoration. Grate the rind from the remaining oranges and squeeze the juice. Cream margarine and sugar; add eggs. Fold in the sieved flour and add the orange rind. Divide the mixture between two 9 inch prepared sandwich tins and bake in the centre of the oven, Mark 4 for 30–35 mins. Brown almonds under the grill.

Sieve icing sugar in a bowl, add butter and beat until light and fluffy. Beat in 2–3 tablesps orange juice. When cakes are thoroughly cold sprinkle orange liqueur over them. Sandwich the cakes together with whipped cream, to which chopped mandarin oranges have been added. Spread ⅓ of the butter icing round the sides of the cake and spike with almonds. Spread the top of the cake with butter icing and put the remainder in an icing bag, fitted with a medium-sized star tube. Decorate with piped butter icing and orange slices cut into halves to make cones or quarters for decorating the top of the cake.

Family dishes for High Tea or Supper, some also suitable for fork supper parties or lunch. A versatile collection of recipes to meet your needs – tasty and satisfying. The younger members of the family will find one or two dishes that they can make themselves.

A few savouries are offered to end this section, ideal to serve with drinks or as the final course for a dinner party.

Halibut Mandarin

4 halibut steaks	*Sauce*
2 tablesps milk	juice of ½ lemon
2 tablesps white wine	1 teasp. water
2 oz margarine	2 egg yolks
1½ lb cooked potatoes	4 oz marg.
mandarin oranges	seasoning

Clean fish and place in dish with milk, wine and margarine. Cover with foil or lid. Bake in oven, Mark 5 for 30 – 35 mins.

Make sauce by placing lemon juice, water and egg yolks in basin over hot water add a little of margarine and whisk until it thickens, remove from heat and gradually add remaining margarine and season.

Pipe potato border round serving dish, brown under grill, place fish in centre, pour over sauce and garnish with orange segments and parsley.

Cod steaks or other white fish can be used, if fillets, these should be rolled up before cooking. **Serves 4**

Corn and Tuna Bake

4 oz sweetcorn	2 eggs (beaten)
3 oz tin of tuna fish (drained)	seasoning
1 onion, finely chopped	1 oz cornflakes
1 tablsp. plain flour	3 oz Cheddar cheese (grated)
½ pt milk	

Mix the sweetcorn, flaked tuna fish and chopped onion together. Blend the flour with the milk and add beaten egg and seasoning. Add the corn mixture to the beaten eggs and milk and pour into an ovenproof dish.

Mix the cornflakes and cheese together and sprinkle over the mixture. Bake at Mark 6 for 40 mins. **Serves 4**

Prawn Roulade

1 oz butter	*Filling*
1 oz flour	2 oz Cheddar cheese (grated)
¼ pt milk	2 oz prawns
3 oz Cheddar cheese (grated)	*Topping* 1 oz grated cheese
3 eggs (separated)	*Garnish* prawns and parsley
seasoning	

Grease a Swiss roll tin and line with greased wax paper. Melt butter in pan, add flour and cook until smooth. Gradually add milk and bring to the boil, stirring. Reduce heat and simmer. Stir until mixture thickens and leaves bottom of pan. Season.

Beat in grated cheese. Whisk in egg yolks and beat mixture well. Whisk egg whites until stiff and fold carefully into mixture.

Pour into greased and lined Swiss roll tin and bake at Mark 4 for 15 mins. Turn out on to greased paper, resting on a damp towel. Remove lining paper and quickly spread over the grated cheese and prawns mixed together. Roll up tightly. Leave for a few mins, then remove paper. Sprinkle over remaining grated cheese and grill until brown. Garnish with prawns and parsley. **Serves 4**

Tuna Risotto

This dish is easily prepared and the finished result is very colourful. Served with a green salad, it makes an ideal luncheon or supper dish.

1 tablesp. oil	1×14 oz can tomatoes
1 chopped onion	1×7 oz can vegetables
4 chopped rashers bacon	1×7½ oz can mushrooms
8 oz long grain rice	1×7 oz can tuna fish
¾ pt stock	

Heat the oil and fry the onion and bacon. Add the rice and fry until fat is absorbed. Stir in the stock, juice from tomatoes and season well. Bring to the boil and simmer for 15 mins. After 10 mins add the chopped tomatoes, vegetables, mushrooms and tuna. Simmer for a further 5 mins and serve hot. **Serves 3 – 4**

Finnan Nests

1 oz butter	$\frac{1}{2}$ pt milk
1 oz flour	salt and pepper
3 tablesps grated cheese	1 teasp. Worcester sauce
creamed potatoes	$\frac{1}{2}$ lb cooked finnan haddock
Garnish Parsley	

Melt butter in pan, stir in flour then gradually add milk, cook until sauce thickens, season with salt, pepper and Worcester sauce. Add grated cheese and cooked, flaked fish. Heat through. Pipe creamed potatoes into four nests. Fill with creamed haddock. Garnish with chopped parsley. **Serves 4**

Country Cheese Bake

1 onion chopped	$\frac{1}{2}$ pt milk
1 carrot chopped	$\frac{1}{2}$ oz flour
1 stick celery chopped	$\frac{1}{2}$ oz margarine
1 oz butter or margarine	2 oz grated cheese
4 cod steaks, $\frac{1}{2}$ inch thick	mashed potato
salt & pepper	

Fry onion, carrot and celery in fat. Put the vegetables in the bottom of an ovenproof dish and lay the cod steaks on top. Make up the cheese sauce and pour over the fish. Pipe or fork the mashed potato round the edge of the dish. Bake at Mark 4 for 25 mins till golden. **Serves 4**

Soused Herring

6 medium sized herring	6 peppercorns
salt and pepper	$\frac{1}{2}$ bay leaf
1 onion	$\frac{3}{4}$ pt white vinegar
2 whole cloves	$\frac{3}{4}$ pt water

Remove head and fins from each fish; scrape off the scales and split open. Clean the inside and remove the backbone. Season with salt and pepper and roll up each fillet, tail first with skin on the outside. Grease a shallow fireproof dish with butter. Place rolled fish into dish and sprinkle over peeled sliced onion, cloves and peppercorns. Add a bay leaf; mix water and vinegar and pour over fish. The fish should be covered with liquid: if insufficient add more water and vinegar. Cover dish with foil and cook in slow oven Mark 2 for 1 hour, remove foil and bake for a further 20 mins. Remove from oven, leave until cold and serve with salad. **Serves 6**

Tacos

12 taco shells	1×15 oz can whole tomatoes
2 tablesps oil	$\frac{1}{4}$ pt water
$1\frac{1}{2}$ lb minced steak	2 tomatoes
1 large onion	6 oz Cheddar cheese
1 clove garlic	2 medium onions, extra
1 teasp. chilli powder	$\frac{1}{2}$ small lettuce
salt and pepper	

Heat oil in frying pan; add meat and peeled and chopped onion; stir until meat is golden brown, mashing meat well. Pour off any surplus fat. Add crushed garlic, chilli powder, salt and pepper; stir 2 mins. Add undrained mashed tomatoes; add water; stir well. Bring to boil; reduce heat;

simmer covered 30 mins; remove lid from pan; simmer uncovered 10 mins or until mixture thickens.

While meat is cooking, cut tomatoes into small pieces; grate cheese; peel and thinly slice extra onions; shred lettuce. Place taco shells on baking tray; bake in moderate oven for 5 mins or until hot.

Guests can assemble their own taco shells. The grated cheese goes in first, then the hot meat mixture (the heat helps melt the cheese); top with tomato, onion and lettuce. If desired, top with a slice of avocado (toss avocado slices in a little lemon juice so they keep their bright colour). **Serves 6**

N.B. Taco shells can be bought in packets of 12 from most supermarkets and food halls.

Lasagne

2×14 oz cans tomatoes, drained	1 oz butter
1 level tablesp. tomato paste	1 oz flour
1 level teasp. dried marjoram	½ pt milk
salt & freshly ground black pepper	6 oz Cheddar cheese, grated
1 lb lean minced beef	oil for glazing
4 oz lasagne strips	4 oz Mozzarella or Bel Paese cheese, sliced

Combine the canned tomatoes, tomato paste, marjoram, salt and pepper. Simmer in an open pan for 30 mins. Add the mince and simmer for a further 25 mins, still uncovered.

Cook the lasagne strips in a large pan of fast boiling, salted water for 10–15 mins and drain.

In small saucepan, melt 1 oz butter, stir in the flour and gradually blend in the milk. Bring to the boil, stirring constantly. Remove from the heat add the Cheddar cheese and season.

Cover the base of an ovenproof dish (about 1½ inch deep) with strips of lasagne. Add alternate layers of meat and cheese sauce. Finish the final layer with strips of pasta placed diagonally across with the sauce spooned between. Lightly oil the pasta to prevent it drying. Bake in oven at Mark 5 for about 30 mins. Remove from the oven, add the slices of Mozzarella on top of the cheese sauce. Raise the temperature to Mark 7 and return the lasagne to the oven until the cheese is golden and bubbling. **Serves 4–6**

Mince and Cheese Crumble

½ lb mince	pinch paprika
1 oz fat	salt & pepper
1 onion	1 tablesp. tomato purée
¼ pt beef stock	2-3 tomatoes
½ oz flour	1 teasp. of sugar
Topping	
2 oz flour	1 oz grated Cheddar cheese
1 oz margarine	salt & pepper

Chop onion and sauté in hot fat, then add mince and brown. Stir in flour and paprika. Blend tomato purée into stock and pour over mince in a casserole. Season and add sugar. Slice tomatoes and lay on top of the meat. For the topping rub margarine into the flour till mixture is like breadcrumbs. Add grated cheese and seasonings. Sprinkle over meat and bake at Mark 5 for 30 mins. **Serves 3**

Pork Peppers

½ lb lean pork	Seasoning
1 onion, peeled and chopped	4 green peppers
1 oz margarine	1 teasp. flour
2 oz mushrooms, sliced	2 tablesps milk

4 oz tomatoes, skinned and diced	Worcester sauce
¼ pt stock	

Dice the pork, melt margarine in pan and gently fry onion and pork for 10 mins, add the sliced mushroom, diced tomato, stock and seasoning, cook slowly for ¾ hour. Blend cornflour with milk, pour into pan, stirring until mixture thickens.

Cut tops off peppers, remove seeds and place in fireproof dish, fill each pepper with pork mixture. Bake in the oven at Mark 5 for 15 mins. Serve with rice or creamed potatoes.
Serves 4

Stuffed Ham with Peach and Watercress Salad

8 oz cheese, grated	1 large bunch watercress
2 level tablesps mayonnaise	4 peaches, skinned, stoned and sliced
4-6 slices cooked ham	3-4 tablesps French dressing
sliced red pepper	salt and pepper

Mix cheese and mayonnaise together and divide between slices of ham and roll up. Toss washed watercress and peach slices together in French dressing and place on serving dish. Arrange ham slices on top and decorate with red pepper rings. Chill before serving. **Serves 4-6**

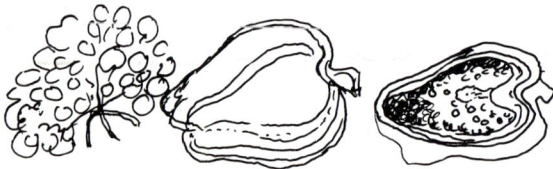

Sausage Plait

1 small pkt frozen puff pastry	3 tablesps tomato ketchup
8 oz pork sausagemeat	1 tablesp. Worcester sauce
1 onion chopped	pinch mixed herbs
4 oz mushrooms sliced	salt and pepper
1 egg beaten	

Roll out pastry to an oblong 14"×12". Mix remaining ingredients together, reserving a little egg for glazing. Spoon the filling down the centre third of pastry leaving a margin top and bottom. Cut diagonal slits ½ inch wide down each side of oblong. Dampen the edges with water. Fold in pastry top and bottom and plait the strips over the filling. Brush with beaten egg. Bake in hot oven Mark 7 for 20 mins then reduce heat to 5 for 10 mins. Serve hot or cold. **Serves 4–6**

Sausage Crunch

A tasty lunch or supper dish using leftover cooked sausages and baked beans.

½ lb sausages, cooked and cut into small pieces	1 tablesp. demerara sugar
1 medium onion, chopped	3 thick slices wholemeal bread
1×7 oz can tomatoes	margarine for spreading
1×2 oz can baked beans in tomato sauce	2 oz Cheddar cheese, grated
1 tablesp. Worcester sauce	
seasoning	

Place sausages in frying pan with onion and fry gently for a few mins. Stir in tomatoes, baked beans, Worcester sauce, sugar and seasoning. Mix well. Pour into a shallow ovenproof dish. Spread both sides of the bread and cut into 1 inch cubes. Cover top of sausage mixture with the bread cubes. Sprinkle cheese on top and bake in centre of oven Mark 6 for approximately 30 mins until top is golden brown and crisp. **Serves 2**

Chicken Pie

1 pkt chicken noodle soup	1 oz butter
1 small onion, chopped	½ pt water
1 lb cooked chicken	1 red apple
1 lb cooked potatoes	chopped parsley

Dice the chicken and mix well with onion. Cook the soup as directed using ½ pint of water. Mix the soup with the chicken and onion and put into a greased pie dish. Mash the potato with the butter and pipe over the chicken. Bake at Mark 6 for 20 mins. Serve garnished with sliced apple and parsley. **Serves 4**

Crispy Drumsticks

1½ oz margarine
2 teasps mustard
3 level tablesps syrup
6 oz parsley and thyme stuffing mix
10 chicken drumsticks

Melt the margarine in a small pan, add the mustard and syrup and stir till well mixed. Put the stuffing mix in a polythene bag. Dip the drumsticks in the pan of liquid and then toss in the mixture in the bag. Place on the rack from your grill pan over the roasting tin and bake at Mark 5 for 40 mins. Serve hot or cold. **Serves 10**

Turkey Tartlets

1 onion finely chopped	¼ pt soured cream
1 oz butter	10 oz cooked turkey, chopped
1×15 oz tin apricot halves	1 teasps. Tabasco sauce
2 teasps curry paste	4 oz frozen peas
2 teasps lemon juice	10 oz puff pastry

Cook the onion in butter till soft and golden brown, add the apricot halves and simmer 20 mins until reduced to a thick pulp. Thin the curry paste with a little water and add to the apricots with the lemon juice. Stir in the soured cream and chopped turkey. Bring to the boil and simmer gently for a further 10 mins. Add the Tabasco sauce and season to taste. Remove from the heat and stir in the peas. Leave to cool till ready for use. Halve the pastry, roll out one half and cut into rounds to line individual patty tins. Divide the cooled turkey mixture between these. Using the remaining pastry, cut rounds to cover the tarts. Pinch the edges together with thumb and forefinger and decorate with pastry leaves. Glaze with beaten egg and cook for 20 mins at Mark 7 until golden brown. **Serves 10**

TWO QUICK SNACKS FOR THE YOUNGER MEMBERS OF THE FAMILY TO MAKE FOR THEMSELVES

Apple Surprise

4 rounds toast	4 apple rings
4 slices luncheon meat	grated cheese
Tomato sauce or chutney	

Put a slice of meat on each round of toast, top with a slice of apple, sprinkle with grated cheese, grill and serve with tomato sauce or chutney. **Serves 4**

Sunshine Susies

4 slices of bread	4 pineapple rings
margarine	4 slices of cheese
chutney	stuffed olives

Toast the bread on one side, spread with margarine and chutney. Lay a pineapple ring on each piece, top with a slice of cheese. Grill until lightly browned and decorate with a piece of olive. **Serves 4**

Cheese and Pickle Pasties

12 oz shortcrust pastry	3 tablesps fresh breadcrumbs
6 oz cheddar cheese, diced	1 eating apple, chopped
2 oz silverskin onions	1 tablesp. redcurrant jelly
2 tablesps chutney	milk to glaze
2 tomatoes, skinned and chopped	

Roll out the pastry thinly and cut into 4 inch rounds. Mix other ingredients together and divide between the rounds of pastry. Damp the edges of the pastry and fold over, seal well by crimping edges with your fingers. Place on a baking sheet with the crimped edges uppermost. Brush with milk to glaze and bake at Mark 6 for 40–45 mins. **Serves 6**

Crusty Mushrooms Rolls

8 oz button mushrooms	2 tablesps chopped parsley
1 oz butter or margarine	salt and freshly ground black pepper
1 level tablesp. flour	2 tablesps sherry
5 fl oz carton single cream	4 large crusty rolls
1 oz melted butter	

Wipe button mushrooms and halve or quarter. Sauté the mushrooms in the butter for 2-3 minutes until well browned. Remove from heat stir in flour, cream, parsley and seasoning. Bring to the boil and simmer gently for 2 mins stirring. Add sherry without reboiling. Cut the tops off the rolls and carefully scoop out the centres, leaving $\frac{1}{4}$ inch thick 'shell'. Brush the inside of the rolls with melted butter, spoon in the warm mushroom filling, replace the tops and bake at Mark 5 for about 15 mins. **Serves 4**

**A FEW QUICK SAVOURIES TO SERVE WITH DRINKS
OR TO END A SPECIAL MEAL**

Chizzi

4 oz plain flour	salt
4 oz margarine	cream cheese
little milk	

Rub fat into flour and salt, bind to a stiff paste with a few drops of milk. Roll out thinly and cut into 2 inch circles. Place a small piece of cream cheese in the centre of a round of pastry, damp the edge and put another round of pastry on top, press the edges firmly together. Continue making cheese and pastry rounds until it is all used. Fry the chizzi in deep hot fat. Drain on kitchen roll. Serve hot. Shallow fat can be used but the pastry rounds require turning. **Serves 10**

Haggis Gabbocks

24 individual bouchée cases	1 lb duchesse potatoes
1 can haggis	$\frac{1}{2}$ lb cooked, mashed turnip

Place a little mashed turnip on the bottom of each bouchée case. Add a layer of haggis and pipe a rosette of duchesse potato on top. Brown in the oven at Mark 5. **Serves 2**

Mussel Savouries

6 oz flaky or shortcrust pastry	juice of 1 lemon
$3\frac{3}{4}$ oz smoked mussels (drained)	

Roll pastry out thinly. Cut out with $1\frac{1}{2}$ inch cutter. Dip mussels in lemon and place on each circle, dampen edges and seal. Fry in deep oil for approximately 5 mins till golden, or bake at Mark 8 for 10 mins. **Serves 10**

Cheese Balls

3 oz butter	$\frac{1}{4}$ teasp. freshly ground black pepper
$\frac{1}{2}$ lb blue cheese	$\frac{1}{2}$ teasp. Worcester sauce
1 tablesp. finely chopped onion	1 teasp. brandy
1 tablesp. finely chopped celery	$\frac{1}{2}$ teasp. paprika
2 tablesp chopped parsley	5 tablesps fine white breadcrumbs

Cream butter and cheese till well blended, then beat in the onion, celery, pepper, Worcester sauce and brandy. Roll into small balls. Mix parsley, paprika and breadcrumbs together in a plastic bag. Toss the balls in the mixture and press in gently. Chill for at least $\frac{1}{2}$ hour before serving. **Serves 10 – 12**

Cheese Logs

8 thin slices of bread, crusts removed

8 thin slices of Cheshire cheese

mustard

5 tablesps melted butter

Spread each piece of bread with mustard and cover with cheese. Roll up and secure with wooden cocktail sticks. Dip each roll in melted butter and bake at Mark 6 for 10 – 15 minutes. **Serves 8 – 16, if halved.**

This chapter offers a selection of menus for complete meals which can be cooked in the oven.

If you are the proud owner of a gas cooker with automatic oven controls you have the added advantage of knowing that when the dishes are prepared and the controls set, you are free to pursue any leisure activity you choose, either at home or miles away.

Catering for a family or entertaining friends, working full, or part-time – automatic cooking by gas will make life easier for you.

The automatic controls are simple and easy to use; they do what you want, when you want it done. Hence the title, 'dial-a-dinner'.

However, not everyone is fortunate enough to have an automatic gas cooker but the menus can still be used, and cooking a whole meal in the oven is so much more economical both in time and money. No frenzied stirring of pots and pans and no steam to wilt the would be hostess. Time to chat to friends over an appetiser before the meal is served – *bon appetit*.

NB: All cooking is from a cold start but if you prefer to pre-heat the oven, deduct 15 minutes from the cooking time.

Menu

Quick Vegetable Soup	Base	Oven setting Mark 4
Stuffed Whiting	Top shelf	Time 45 mins
Duchesse Potatoes	Lower shelf	
Tomato Casserole	Lower shelf	
Caramel Pears	Top shelf	
Serves 2		

Quick Vegetable Soup

1 carrot, grated	1 leek, diced finely
small piece of turnip, grated	1 pt stock
1 stick of celery, diced finely	

Bring all to the boil, reduce gas, and simmer for 10 minutes. Transfer to casserole, or ovenproof bowl and cover

Stuffed Whiting

3 fillets of whiting	1 oz margarine
3 tablesps breadcrumbs	rind and juice of 1 lemon
1 small onion, finely chopped	1 egg
1 oz mushrooms, finely chopped	seasoning
3 rashers streaky bacon	

Cut the fillets in half, lengthwise and the rashers either lengthwise or across the way. Mix all other ingredients together. Put a spoonful of the mixture on each skinned side of fish fillet and roll up from head to tail. Wrap the bacon round and secure with a skewer or wooden cocktail stick. Place in an ovenproof dish and dot with margarine.

Duchesse Potatoes

1 lb potatoes, cooked & mashed	salt & pepper
1 egg	pinch of allspice

Add beaten egg, seasoning and a slight pinch of allspice to potatoes and beat till smooth. Pipe on to a greased Swiss roll tin or put on in spoonfuls.

Tomato Casserole

2 large tomatoes, sliced	pinch of salt & pepper
2 oz cheese, grated	2 oz potato crisps, crushed
1 oz onion, very finely sliced	

Place in casserole a layer of tomato followed by a layer of cheese and onion, seasoning each layer. Repeat until all has been used. Cover with crushed crisps.

Caramel Pears

1 lb pears, peeled & quartered	1 tablesp. water
1 oz soft brown sugar	2 tablesps double cream lightly whipped
1 oz butter	

Arrange the pears in an ovenproof dish. Sprinkle with sugar and dot with butter. Sprinkle on the water. Once removed from the oven, pour over the cream.

Menu

Green Pea Soup	Base	Oven setting Mark 4
Washington Chops	Lower shelf	
Baked French Potatoes	Top shelf	Time 1 Hour
Austrian Rice Pudding	Base	
Serves 4		

Green Pea Soup

10 oz pkt frozen peas	$1\frac{1}{2}$ oz margarine
2 chicken stock cubes	$\frac{1}{4}$ pt double cream
$1\frac{1}{2}$ pts boiling water	seasoning
$\frac{1}{4}$ teasp. sugar	pinch of ground nutmeg
1 oz flour	

Cook peas in measured water with stock cubes and sugar, liquidise. Melt fat, stir in flour, blend in purée and bring to boil. Add nutmeg and seasoning, place in heat resistant dish, cover with foil and put on base of oven. Before serving stir in cream.

Washington Casserole

4 pork chops	$\frac{1}{4}$ cup water
$\frac{1}{4}$ teasp. curry powder	4 prunes
$\frac{1}{2}$ teasp. salt	8 apricot slices
1 cup orange juice	watercress to garnish

Remove fat from chops, brown chops on both sides. Mix curry powder and salt, blend in orange juice and water. Pour over chops. Place fruit on top, cover casserole and put in oven (runner position 4th from top).

Baked French Potatoes

$1\frac{1}{2}$ lb potatoes	2 oz melted margarine

Peel and slice potatoes. Place in a dish and pour melted margarine over. Season well. Cover and place in oven (2nd runner position from top).

Austrian Rice Pudding

2 oz rice	2 oz butter
1 pt milk	4 oz sugar
grated rind of $\frac{1}{2}$ lemon	2 eggs

Simmer rice in milk until soft. Cream butter and sugar, add lemon rind and beaten egg yolks. Mix with rice, fold in stiffly beaten egg whites. Bake on base of oven.

Menu

Mushroom Soup	Lower shelf	Oven setting Mark 6
Viennese Chicken	Top shelf	Time 45 mins
Savoury Rice	Top shelf	
Devilled Sauce	Oven base	
Apple Rum Meringue	Oven base	
Serves 4		

Mushroom Soup

1 oz butter	1 small onion, finely chopped
1 oz flour	1 tablesp. chopped parsley
4 oz mushrooms, finely chopped	salt & freshly ground black pepper
¾ pt chicken stock	1 dessertsp. lemon juice
¾ pt milk	2 tablesps double cream

Put all the ingredients, except the lemon juice and cream, into a large saucepan. Whisking continuously, bring to the boil, place in an ovenproof casserole, cover and cook on the lower shelf in the oven at Mark 6 for 45 mins. Before serving add the lemon juice and cream. Stir well and serve at once. This can be cooked on the hotplate, after bringing to the boil, simmer for 10 minutes.

Viennese Chicken

4 chicken breasts	2 oz Parmesan cheese
3 oz fresh white breadcrumbs	salt & freshly ground black pepper
1 tablesp. parsley, chopped	6 oz butter
1 teasp. basil	shake of garlic salt
1 lemon, finely grated	

Skin the chicken joints. Combine the breadcrumbs, herbs, lemon rind, seasoning and Parmesan cheese. Melt half the butter with the garlic. Dip the joints in melted butter (beaten egg could be used) then in the breadcrumb mixture, pressing the crumbs on well. Place the chicken joints in an ovenproof dish and pour round the remaining butter. Bake on the top shelf at Mark 6 for 45 mins. This can be cooked on the hotplate. Fry the chicken gently in melted butter for 25 mins or until cooked.

Savoury Rice

8 oz long grain rice	1½ teasps salt
1 small tin sweetcorn with peppers	¾ pt chicken stock
few strands saffron	

Drain tin of sweetcorn. Put all the ingredients into an ovenproof casserole, cover and cook on the top shelf at Mark 6 for 45 mins. The rice should absorb the water and should not need draining or rinsing. Just fork up and serve with the chicken. This can also be cooked on the hotplate in the usual way.

Devilled Sauce

3 tablesps tomato purée	1 teasp. garlic salt
¼ pt water	1 teasp. chilli seasoning
2 tablesps tomato and chilli chutney	1½ teasps Worcester sauce
1 tablesp. made mustard	1 tablesp. sugar

Blend all ingredients together well. Place in ovenproof sauce boat, cook on the base of the oven at Mark 6 for 45 mins. If cooking on the hotplate, just leave the sauce to simmer for 5 mins.

Apple Rum Meringue

4 oz ratafia biscuits	4 oz soft brown sugar
4 tablesps Bacardi rum	3 egg whites
1½ lb cooking apples	¼ level teasp. salt
1 oz butter	6 oz caster sugar
½ level teasp. of cinnamon	glacé cherries for decoration

Cover the base of an ovenproof pie or flan dish with the ratafias and pour the rum over them. Peel, core and finely slice the apples into a saucepan. Add the butter, cinnamon, brown sugar and 2–3 tablesps of water. Simmer for 10–15 mins or until the apples are just cooked. Leave to cool, then spoon the apples over the base. Beat the egg whites with the salt until stiff, but not dry. Beat in gradually two thirds of the caster sugar and fold in the remaining one third, reserving a little for dredging. Spoon or pipe the meringue over the apples. Dredge with remaining caster sugar, and decorate with glacé cherries. Place on the base of the oven and bake at Mark 6 for 45 mins. Serve hot or cold.

Menu

Baked Grapefruit	Base	
Chicken in a Parcel	Top shelf	Oven setting Mark 5
French Beans	Lower shelf	Time 1 hour
Baked Potatoes	Top shelf	
Lemon Delight	Lower shelf	
Serves 2		

Baked grapefruit

1 grapefruit, halved & segmented	2 teasps sherry (optional)
2 teasps demerara sugar	1 glacé cherry

Sprinkle the sugar and sherry over the grapefruit halves and put a half cherry in the centre of each. Place on an entrée dish on the base of the oven.

Chicken in a Parcel

2 chicken joints	2 tablesps cider
2 tablesps mustard	2 tablesps honey or marmalade

Cut two pieces of foil large enough to wrap the chicken in. Skin the joints and place on foil. Mix honey, cider and mustard together. Spoon the mixture over the chicken and fold each up into a loose parcel. Place on a baking tray on top shelf of oven.

French Beans

½ lb frozen beans	½ oz butter or margarine
salt & pepper	

Cut a square of tin foil, to take beans. Rub butter over foil, place beans on and season. Wrap up into a loose parcel and place on lower oven shelf.

Baked Potatoes

4 small-sized potatoes, washed	4 skewers
oil	

Rub the oil over the potato skin. Pierce through with a skewer and place on top shelf.

Lemon Delight

1 oz margarine	1 egg
2 oz sugar	rind & juice of 1 lemon
1 tablesp. S.R. flour	¼ pt milk

Cream the fat and sugar and beat in the egg yolk, rind and juice. Fold in the flour and add the milk. Whisk the egg white till stiff and fold in. Turn into a buttered 6 inch soufflé dish and set in a shallow tin of water on the lower shelf.

Menu

Liver Française	Lower shelf	Oven setting Mark 5
Minted Peas	Base	Time 1 hour
Pommes Anna	Top shelf	
Raspberry Soufflé	Base	Serves 4

Liver Française

¾ lb lambs liver	1 tablesp. parsley, chopped
4 rashers of streaky bacon, halved	salt & pepper
½ pt stock	pinch of ground allspice
1 dessertsp. Worcester sauce	egg to bind
2 oz breadcrumbs	

Wash the liver well and dry it. Grease an ovenproof dish and lay on the 8 pieces of liver. Mix the breadcrumbs, parsley, salt and pepper and allspice and bind with an egg. Spread on to each piece of liver and cover with a piece of bacon. Pour the stock and Worcester Sauce round. Place on lower shelf in oven.

Minted Peas

¾ lb frozen peas	margarine
1 tablesp. mint jelly	salt & pepper

Cut a square of tinfoil large enough to take the peas. Rub this with margarine. Put on peas and mint jelly. Season and fold up into a parcel. Place on base of oven.

Pommes Anna

1 lb peeled potatoes	salt and pepper
butter or dripping, melted	

Cut the potatoes wafer thin. Grease a 7 inch or 8 inch round cake tin. Lay an overlapping layer of potatoes in the base, season, and brush with melted fat. Continue in this manner till all the potatoes are used. Bake on top shelf of oven.

Raspberry Soufflé

1 lb raspberries, mashed,	$\frac{1}{8}$ pt double cream
keep 4 for decoration and a few leaves	2 oz white breadcrumbs
3 oz caster sugar	2 oz ground rice
2 large eggs, separated	a little butter

Whisk the egg whites stiffly. Mix all the other ingredients into the fruit. Fold in the stiffly beaten egg whites. Lightly butter a deep 6 inch soufflé dish and dust with a little sugar. Put in the mixture and place on the base of the oven. When cooked, cool slightly before turning out and decorate with the whole berries and leaves.

I/M/P/E/R/I/A/L M/E/T/R/I/C
C/O/M/P/A/R/I/S/O/N/S G/U/I/D/E

Weights

Imperial	Metric
$\frac{1}{2}$oz	15g
1oz	25g
4oz	100g
6oz	175g
8oz	225g
1lb	450g
2.2lb	1kg

Fluid Measures

Imperial	Fluid	Metric
$\frac{1}{4}$ pt	5 fl oz	125ml
$\frac{1}{2}$ pt	10 fl oz	250ml
$\frac{3}{4}$ pt	15 fl oz	375ml
1 pt	20 fl oz	500ml
$1\frac{3}{4}$ pt		1 litre

Spoon Measures

Spoon	Metric
1 teasp.	5ml
1 desstsp.	10ml
1 tablesp.	15ml

Baking and Roasting Tins

6 inch for 15cm
$6\frac{1}{2}$ inch for 16cm
7 inch for 18cm
8 inch for 20cm
10 inch for 25cm

U/S/I/N/G Y/O/U/R G/A/S O/V/E/N

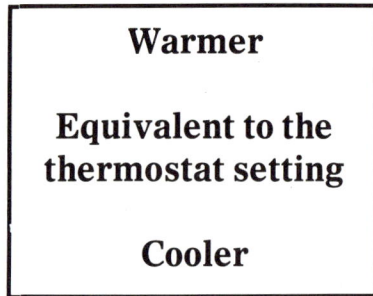

Warmer

**Equivalent to the
thermostat setting**

Cooler

Zones of heat

One of the many advantages of a British gas oven are the
zones of heat. The middle of the oven is equivalent to the
thermostat setting. It is warmer above and cooler below. By
using these zones of heat, food requiring different
thermostat settings can be cooked together in the oven at the
same time.

Shelf positions

Gas ovens usually have two shelves and between 4 – 7 shelf
runners. The runner positions are counted from the top
downwards. The base of the oven can also be used to cook
certain foods.

N.B. Always leave at least one runner position between
shelves.

Baking trays

A baking tray and roasting tin are provided with the cooker
and these are the largest that should be used for even baking.
However when roasting use a tin appropriate to the size of
the joint. This reduces splashing of the oven interior.
Rectangular trays and tins should always be placed
according to the manufacturer's instructions.

Pre-heating

Gas ovens heat up very quickly and so it is not necessary to
pre-heat the oven before cooking, except for very sensitive
dishes.

Manufacturer's instructions

To help you get the best results from your cooker the
manufacturer provides an instruction book which gives
detailed information on the use of the oven, hob and grill,
care and cleaning of the cooker and information on any
special features. It is important to read it very carefully and
keep it handy for easy reference. However if you need
further advice on the use of your gas cooker, please contact
the Home Service Adviser, through your local gas showroom
or service centre.

F/U/E/L S/A/V/I/N/G H/I/N/T/S

1. Put lids on saucepans.
2. Use correct size of saucepan and reduce flame under the base.
3. Turn gas down as soon as pan boils.
4. Do not overfill kettles or pans – boil only what is necessary.
5. Consider cooking a complete meal in your Pressure Cooker.
6. Consider cooking a complete meal in your oven.
7. Let warm food cool down before putting into the fridge or freezer.
8. Do not open the refrigerator/freezer door unnecessarily and do not leave open.
9. Defrost the refrigator and freezer regularly.
10. Do not wash up under a running tap.
11. Repair dripping taps.
12. Use time clocks to control heating and hot water.
13. New appliances burn more efficiently than old ones.
14. Have your appliances serviced regularly to ensure efficient running – service contracts are available from Scottish Gas.
15. Preheating the grill is not necessary.
Don't turn on the oven just to brown a dish, use the grill. Try cooking a complete meal under the grill.

16. Remember appliances need air to work efficiently and safely – some ventilation is important for health and comfort.
17. No need to preheat the oven, just add approx. 15 mins longer for cooking time.
18. Potatoes and vegetables cut small, cook quicker.
19. Don't keep opening the oven door during cooking.
20. One therm of gas will run an oven at Mark 2 for 36 hours.
21. The base of the oven can be used for heating things through.
22. One therm of gas will run an oven at Mark 7 for 20 hours.
23. Pressure Cookers save energy and time.
24. Don't use your oven to cook one dish only, make full use of it.
25. Always leave at least one runner position free between oven shelves, to allow heat to circulate.
26. Don't use oven trays larger than those provided with cooker, or scorching will occur round the edges.
27. 1 therm of gas will run a fridge for 7 days.
28. 1 therm of gas will run a fridge/freezer for 5 days.
29. Keep all foods covered in your fridge.
30. Gas ovens are heat graded – hotter at top, cooler at bottom.

H/A/N/D/Y H/I/N/T/S

1. Boil apple peelings in badly stained saucepans to remove stains.

2. Skin peels off a tomato easily if it is held on a fork over a gas flame.

3. Wear a plastic or rubber glove to give grip when unscrewing bottles or jars.

4. To remove a cake from a loose-bottomed cake tin – stand the tin on a jar and push down the sides gently to release.

5. New baking tins should be well greased and then heated in the oven for 15 mins to prevent future rusting.

6. To freshen stale bread – wrap tightly in foil and place in oven (Mark 8) for 5 mins then allow to cool in foil.

7. Frozen herbs are easily crumbled without chopping when being added to food.

8. To make whipped cream go further fold in the stiffly beaten white of egg.

9. If a pan goes on fire – DO NOT LIFT IT and DO NOT POUR WATER ON IT. TURN OFF HEAT IMMEDIATELY and smother the flames by placing a lid or large plate on the pan.

G/U/I/D/E T/O O/V/E/N S/E/T/T/I/N/G/S

Follow the manufacturer's instructions for lighting the oven and turn the thermostat control to 9 before setting at the appropriate gas mark. The thermostat will maintain the oven at a constant temperature throughout the cooking period.

When a different setting to that shown here is given in a recipe, the recipe instructions should be followed.

The thermostat setting refers to the middle of the oven, it is warmer above and cooler below, see 'Zones of heat' overleaf.

Some ovens have a special low thermostat setting which is below mark $\frac{1}{4}$. It is used for cooking food slowly over a long period, eg. casseroles.

	Heat of Oven	Thermostat Settings	Approximate Electric Oven Temperatures	
Plate warming	very cool	$\frac{1}{4}$	225°F	110°C
Keeping food hot prior to serving. Meringues	very cool	$\frac{1}{2}$	250°F	120°C
Milk puddings, egg custard stewing fruit	cool	1	275°F	140°C
Rich fruit cakes	cool	2	300°F	150°C
Low temperature roasting, casseroles, shortbread	moderate	3	325°F	160°C
Victoria sandwich, ginger bread, plain fruit cake	moderate	4	350°F	180°C
Small cakes, baking fish	fairly hot	5	375°F	190°C
Short crust pastry, soufflés, choux pastry	fairly hot	6	400°F	200°C
High temperature roasting, flaky pastry, scones, batters, swiss roll	hot	7	425°F	220°C
Puff pastry, bread	very hot	8	450°F	230°C
Quick browning of cooked foods	very hot	9	475°F	240°C

I / N / D / E / X

Notes

Notes

Notes

Notes

Notes

Notes